School Subject-Integrated Reading Series

Reading for

SECOND EDITION

Subject

4

Reading for Subject 4

Publisher Chung Kyudo
Authors Ko Miseon, Kim Seungmi, Kim Haeja, Yu Sunyeh,
Han Jiyoung, Rachel Somer
Editors Jeong Yeonsoon, Seo Jeong-ah
Designer Koo Soojung

First published in December 2021
By Darakwon, Inc.
Darakwon Bldg., 211, Munbal-ro, Paju-si, Gyeonggi-do 10881
Republic of Korea
Tel: 82-2-736-2031 (Ext. 250)
Fax: 82-2-732-2037

Copyright © 2021 Plus Edu., Inc

All rights reserved. No part of this publication may be reproduced,
stored in a retrieval system, or transmitted in any form or by any
means, electronic, mechanical, photocopying or otherwise, without
the prior consent of the copyright owner. Refund after purchase is
possible only according to the company regulations. Contact the
above telephone number for any inquiries. Consumer damages
caused by loss, damage, etc. can be compensated according
to the consumer dispute resolution standards announced by the
Korea Fair Trade Commission. An incorrectly collated book will be
exchanged.

ISBN 978-89-277-0899-5 54740
978-89-277-0895-7 54740 (set)

www.darakwon.co.kr

Photo Credits
Grisha Bruev (p.10), dmitro2009 (p.11), Nopparat Khokthong (p.22),
AngieYeoh (p.26), Nuamfolio (p.38), Blueee77 (p.39), ymphotos
(p.51), spatuletail (p.59), structuresxx (p.67), ALLYOU Grzegorz
Wasowicz (p.74), ID1974 (p.75), Anna Pakutina (p.94)
/ www.shutterstock.com
Canestra di frutta (Caravaggio) (p.95) / https://commons.wikimedia.
org/wiki/

Components Main Book / Workbook
9 8 7 6 5 4 3   24 25 26 27 28

School Subject-Integrated Reading Series

Reading for Subject

SECOND EDITION

4

How to Use This Book

This book has 5 chapters, and each consists of 4 units. At the end of a chapter, there is a writing activity with a topic related to the last unit.

Student Book

QR code for listening to the reading passage

Finding the topic of each paragraph

Two warm-up questions to encourage students to think about the topic of the unit

BEFORE YOU READ

Students can learn the meaning of key vocabulary words by matching the words with their definitions.

Background knowledge about the topic is provided to help students better understand the main reading passage.

MAIN READING PASSAGE

Interesting, informative nonfiction reading passages covering various school subjects are provided.

CHECK YOUR COMPREHENSION

This section asks students to identify the main ideas and details and to make accurate inferences from the passage through 4 multiple-choice and 2 short-answer questions.

SHOW YOUR COMPREHENSION

Students can remember what they have read and organize the key information in the passage in a visual manner.

SUMMARIZE YOUR READING

Students can review and practice summarizing the key information in the passage.

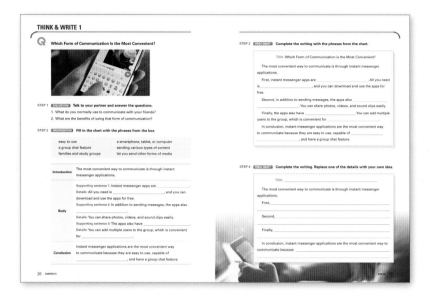

THINK & WRITE

Students can strengthen their writing skills by connecting ideas from the passage to their own lives. This also helps students prepare themselves for English performance assessments in school.

Students can review the vocabulary they learn in each unit. They can also review key structures in the passages by translating sentences and by putting words in the correct order.

Table of Contents

UNIT 01

Subject Art & Music
Topic Busking

The World Is a Stage

WARM UP

1. What types of street performance have you seen?
2. If you could perform on the street, what would you do?

BEFORE YOU READ

A   Match the words with the definitions below.

1. _____ in public
2. _____ acrobatics
3. _____ entertain
4. _____ break into
5. _____ means
6. _____ steady

a. a way to do something
b. to enter a certain industry
c. continuous; without stopping
d. the skills of a performer at a circus
e. to make people enjoy themselves
f. in a place where many people can see you

B   Background Knowledge

Street performance is one of the longest surviving entertainment traditions in the world. In fact, there is evidence that street performers were common in Ancient Egypt, Rome, and India. In the Middle Ages, merchants hired street performers to attract business. Later, in America, performers joined circuses. But as circuses fell out of popularity, performers went back to the streets to share their talents.

Street performance has been around for thousands of years. However, it wasn't until the 1860s that street performance got its name, busking. Busking is the act of performing **in public** for tips. Parks, streets, and even subway stations are all popular busking
5   locations nowadays. Buskers visit these places during times of heavy foot traffic and perform in a variety of ways. If observers enjoy the performances, they might offer tips in the form of money, food, or gifts.

There are numerous
10 types of busking. Some buskers perform dance numbers. Others might engage in more dangerous displays, such as **acrobatics**,
15 while some entertainers perform as jugglers, clowns,

or living statues. One of the most popular forms of busking is musical performance. Classical musicians might gather with their instruments to perform. Similarly, modern bands and folk singers
20 might **entertain** crowds with their own original songs.

Busking is an appealing opportunity for performers. Not all performers can find work. For a clown or an acrobat, it may be difficult to get a job. For musicians, it can be difficult to **break into** the music industry and many do not pass auditions. However,
25 busking offers them a **means** to do what they love and make a little money doing so. Furthermore, busking is a great way for performers and audience members alike to exchange culture and ideas.

It is not always easy being a busker, however, and many buskers
30 have trouble making a **steady** income. If the weather is poor, they might not be able to perform. Sometimes, they simply do not make enough tips to support themselves. Additionally, not everyone is friendly to buskers, and some see busking as begging for money. Still, many buskers remain hopeful, knowing that artists like Ed
35 Sheeran and Robin Williams successfully busked their way to fame and fortune.   Words 301

Q

What is the paragraph mainly about?

P1 How _____
is done

P2 The numerous (places / types) of busking

P3 The (benefits / difficulties) of being a busker

P4 Why busking is not always
_____

CHECK YOUR COMPREHENSION

Choose the best answers.

<u>Main idea</u>   1   **What is the main idea of the passage?**

   a. Busking has changed significantly since it began.

   b. Busking is the best way to break into the music industry.

   c. There are more buskers now than there were in the past.

   d. Busking is an art form with positives and negatives.

<u>Details</u>   2   **Which is NOT true about busking according to the passage?**

   a. Busking got its name in the 1860s.

   b. Buskers always get tips in the form of money.

   c. Buskers perform in busy areas when many people are around.

   d. Musical performance is one of the most popular types of busking.

3   **According to the passage, which is NOT a way busking benefits performers?**

   a. It helps them pass industry auditions.

   b. It helps them do what they love.

   c. It gives them a way to make some money.

   d. It allows them to exchange ideas with an audience.

4   **Some people are _____ to buskers, and some view busking as _____ .**

   a. friendly – noise

   b. unfriendly – noise

   c. friendly – begging for money

   d. unfriendly – begging for money

Write the answers in complete sentences.

5   **Where does busking take place nowadays?**

   _____

6   **What do many buskers have trouble doing?**

   _____

SHOW YOUR COMPREHENSION

Fill in the chart with the phrases from the box.

Busking

Types of Busking	• some dance or ❶_____ • some perform as jugglers, clowns, or living statues • musical performance is one of ❷_____

The Benefits	• a means for entertainers to do what they love and
	  ❸_____
	• allows performers to ❹_____ with
	  an audience

The Difficulties	• difficult to make a steady income through busking • some are unfriendly to buskers and ❺_____

engage in acrobatics	exchange culture and ideas
make a little money	some see it as begging	the most popular types

SUMMARIZE YOUR READING

Complete the summary with the words from the box.

easy	many types	in public	fortune
find work	appealing	living statues	support

Busking is the act of performing ❶_____ for tips. There are ❷_____ of busking. Some buskers are dancers, jugglers, or clowns. Others engage in acrobatics or perform as ❸_____. One of the most popular types of busking is musical performance. Busking is a(n) ❹_____ option for many performers. It can be difficult to ❺_____ as a performer, but busking lets entertainers do what they love and make a little money. However, life is not always ❻_____ for buskers. They often don't make enough money to ❼_____ themselves. But many are hopeful that busking will bring them fame and ❽_____.

UNIT 02 |

Subject Math
Topic The Fibonacci Sequence

Magic Numbers in the Universe

WARM UP

1. What is the shape of a galaxy?
2. Name some other things in nature that also have this shape.

BEFORE YOU READ

A Match the words with the definitions below.

1. _____ sequence   a. a possible effect or result

2. _____ assumption   b. to produce young animals or plants

3. _____ reproduce   c. coming or happening one after another

4. _____ infinity   d. a number that is too large to be calculated

5. _____ successive   e. the place or thing that something comes from

6. _____ source   f. a series of things or events that are related to each other

B Background Knowledge

The golden ratio is a math concept that describes a ratio of 1 to 1.618. When found in nature, the golden ratio can create spiral patterns such as those found in fruit, vegetables, and flowers. However, the ratio can also be seen in the human face, hands, etc. The golden ratio is considered beautiful, and many famous artists have used it in their paintings.

The Fibonacci **sequence** is a set of numbers that can be found everywhere. It was named after an Italian mathematician, Leonardo of Pisa, now known as Fibonacci. In 1202, he wrote *The Book of Calculation* in which he first shared the number pattern with
5　Western Europe.

　　Fibonacci first noticed the sequence while trying to answer the following question: how many rabbits could be produced from a single pair in one year? He made a few **assumptions** to solve the problem. First, he imagined two newborn rabbits, one male
10　and one female, were placed in a field. Second, he noted that the rabbits would not **reproduce** until they were one month old. Lastly, he theorized that a grownup female could give birth to a new pair of rabbits of different sexes each month, and that the rabbits never died.

15　　　Following these assumptions, the original female would give birth to a new pair at the end of the second month. So there were two pairs. In the third month, there were three pairs since the original female produced another pair while the new pair born in the second month grew up. Thus, the number of pairs in the field at
20　the start of each month was 1, 1, 2, 3, 5, 8, 13, 21, 34, 55, 89...

These numbers go on and on to **infinity**. Interestingly, Fibonacci found that each number in the sequence is the
25　sum of the two previous numbers. He also found that the ratio between the **successive** numbers is about 1.618. This is known as the golden ratio. When represented visually, it implies
30　that everything in life spirals outward from one **source**.

　　The golden ratio appears in various forms in nature. For instance, the number of petals in a flower and the spiral pattern in a pinecone both reflect the Fibonacci sequence and the golden ratio. The same is true for the way tree branches split and the spiral shape of a galaxy. **Words 325**

Q

What is the paragraph mainly about?

P1　The work of
_____

P2　The _____
Fibonacci tried to answer

P3　The (test / results) of the rabbit problem

P4　(What / How) Fibonacci found

P5　The golden ratio in
_____

CHECK YOUR COMPREHENSION

Choose the best answers.

Main idea **1** **What is the passage mainly about?**

　　a. The use of mathematics in everyday life

　　b. Fibonacci's contributions to mathematics

　　c. Interesting facts about the reproductive habits of rabbits

　　d. The discovery of the Fibonacci sequence and how it works

Details **2** **Which is NOT an assumption made by Fibonacci in his research?**

　　a. At the start of the first month, there was a pair of newborn rabbits.

　　b. Each pair of rabbits consisted of one male and one female.

　　c. A mature female rabbit gave birth to one rabbit each month.

　　d. The rabbits could not reproduce until they were one month old.

3 **Fibonacci found the Fibonacci sequence** _____.

　　a. by carrying out experiments on various plants

　　b. by trying to figure out the golden ratio in nature

　　c. by observing young rabbit pairs he bred in a field

　　d. by solving a math problem involving rabbit reproduction

4 **Which is NOT true about the golden ratio?**

　　a. It is approximately 1.618.

　　b. It can create spiral patterns.

　　c. It was named by Leonardo Fibonacci.

　　d. It occurs in many forms in nature.

Write the answers in complete sentences.

5 **What things in nature reflect the Fibonacci sequence and the golden ratio?**

_____

6 **What does the golden ratio imply when represented visually?**

_____

SHOW YOUR COMPREHENSION

Fill in the chart with the phrases from the box.

The Fibonacci Sequence	
Discovery	• found by ❶_____, Leonardo Fibonacci • He tried to determine ❷_____ that could be produced from a single pair.
What It Is	• Each number is the sum of the ❸_____. • The ratio between any successive numbers is about 1.618 and is ❹_____.
Representations in Nature	• ❺_____ in a flower, the spiral pattern of a pinecone, the way tree branches split, and the spiral shape of a galaxy

> the number of rabbit pairs   an Italian mathematician
> called the golden ratio   two previous numbers   the number of petals

SUMMARIZE YOUR READING

Complete the summary with the words from the box.

> found   nature   previous two   sequence
> assumptions   successive   be produced   characteristics

In 1202, Italian mathematician Leonardo Fibonacci shared a number ❶_____

in *The Book of Calculation*. He found this sequence while trying to answer the following

question: how many rabbits could ❷_____ from a single pair in a year?

Basing his calculations on a few ❸_____, Fibonacci solved the problem and

❹_____ a number sequence which is now known as the Fibonacci sequence.

He also found the numbers had some interesting ❺_____. Each number is

the sum of the ❻_____, and the ratio between any two ❼_____

numbers is about 1.618. This is called the golden ratio and is represented in

❽_____ in various ways.

From Bright to White

WARM UP

1. What colors do you prefer to wear, and why?
2. If you get married someday, what color will you wear?

BEFORE YOU READ

A Match the words with the definitions below.

1. _____ engagement
2. _____ bold
3. _____ combine
4. _____ purity
5. _____ option
6. _____ naturally

a. very bright and strong in color
b. obviously; not at all surprisingly
c. to mix two different things together
d. a formal agreement to get married
e. the state of being clean or innocent
f. a choice you can make in a particular situation

B Background Knowledge

A wedding ceremony is an official event that happens when a couple decides to get married. Some wedding ceremonies are religious events that also celebrate the couple's faith. Non-religious weddings are often held in hotels, wedding halls, parks, or on beaches. Most wedding ceremonies are followed by a reception in which the guests gather to celebrate.

Weddings in the past used to be quite different from how they are nowadays. Many times, they were not about romantic **engagements** but were political matters for nobles and members of the upper class. Accordingly, the dresses the brides wore were seen
5 as symbols of their families' wealth. It was also common for brides from wealthy families to wear colorful dresses instead of white ones.

Back then, wearing **bold** color wedding dresses was natural, and it still is in some
10 Eastern cultures. In China and India, brides wear red wedding dresses or a combination of red and white. In these cultures, the color red is seen as a symbol of good luck and wealth. In Japan, brides often wear more
15 than just one dress throughout the ceremony. Typically, they **combine** colored dresses with one white dress.

In Western cultures, the first wedding dresses were blue, for the color was seen as a symbol of **purity**. Brides also wore brightly
20 colored dresses to show their happiness. Often, they would wear dresses they already owned. If they bought new dresses, they made sure they could wear them again. White was not a popular **option** because it was not an easy color to keep clean.

It was not until 1840, when England's Queen Victoria got married
25 to Albert of Saxe-Coburg and Gotha, that white wedding dresses became popular. Even though it was not common to wear the color white, when other women saw the queen's color choice, they **naturally** followed. Wearing the color white then became regarded as a symbol of wealth.

30 Soon, the white wedding dress became popular with brides not only in Western cultures but also in Eastern ones. For some, wearing a white wedding dress is still seen as a symbol of purity and wealth. But for many others, the color has lost all meaning and is merely something worn for tradition's sake. Words 312

Q

What is the paragraph mainly about?

P1 (Where / Why) weddings took place in the past

P2 Wedding dress colors in _____ cultures

P3 The first wedding dresses in _____ cultures

P4 How the (blue / white) wedding dress became popular

P5 What it means to wear a (white / queen's) wedding dress nowadays

CHECK YOUR COMPREHENSION

Choose the best answers.

Main idea 1 **What is the passage mainly about?**

   a. The history of royal weddings

   b. Wedding cultures around the world

   c. The history of the white wedding dress

   d. The meanings of colored wedding dresses

Details 2 **In the past, brides wore colorful dresses because they wanted to**

   _____ .

   a. save money

   b. show off their wealth

   c. sell the dresses after

   d. pretend to be queens

3 **According to paragraph 3, which is NOT true about wedding dresses in Western cultures?**

   a. The first wedding dresses were not white.

   b. Brides chose bright colors to show they were happy.

   c. Brides combined colored dresses with one white dress.

   d. Brides would wear their wedding dresses more than once.

4 **What can be inferred from the passage?**

   a. Colored wedding dresses are no longer worn by brides.

   b. The purpose of wedding ceremonies has not changed.

   c. Wearing a white wedding dress has been popular since the 19th century.

   d. Wearing a white dress became popular because it was a symbol of good luck.

Write the answers in complete sentences.

5 **Why do brides in China and India wear red wedding dresses?**

   _____

6 **Why was white initially not a popular color for wedding dresses in Western cultures?**

   _____

SHOW YOUR COMPREHENSION

Fill in the chart with the phrases from the box.

	The White Wedding Dress
In Eastern Cultures	• China and India: wear red or ❶ _____ • Japan: wear colored dresses along with one white dress
In Western Cultures	• The first wedding dresses were blue, which symbolized purity. • Brides wore bright colors to ❷ _____. • White was not popular because it was ❸ _____ _____.
White Wedding Dress	• became popular after ❹ _____ • is now seen as a symbol of purity and wealth for some, but for others, it ❺ _____

difficult to keep clean   a combination of red and white

has lost all meaning   show their happiness   Queen Victoria's wedding

SUMMARIZE YOUR READING

Complete the summary with the words from the box.

popular   wealth   white   common

colorful dresses   purity   good luck   the color blue

Wearing white during a wedding was not a ❶ _____ tradition in the past. Back then, the dress a bride wore represented the ❷ _____ of her family. Therefore, it was common for brides to wear ❸ _____. In Eastern cultures, wearing the color red is still seen as a symbol of ❹ _____ and wealth. In Western cultures, originally, ❺ _____ was a symbol of purity while the color ❻ _____ was not a popular option. This was because white is a difficult color to keep clean. White wedding dresses became ❼ _____ only after Queen Victoria wore one at her wedding. Today, some see a white wedding dress as a symbol of ❽ _____ and wealth, but many do not.

UNIT 04 |
Subject Language
Topic Translation Apps

Translating for the Future

WARM UP
1. What types of apps do you normally use?
2. How have translation apps helped you?

BEFORE YOU READ

A **Match the words with the definitions below.**

1. _____ barrier   a. to use in an effective way
2. _____ application   b. an aspect or part of something
3. _____ physical   c. a piece of software designed for a purpose
4. _____ utilize   d. relating to things that you can see or touch
5. _____ mistranslation   e. an incorrect translation from one language to another
6. _____ element   f. a thing that prevents people from understanding each other

B **Background Knowledge**

A language barrier is the inability to communicate when people do not speak the same language. Nowadays, English is considered the global language of business. However, there are billions of people who do not speak English. In fact, over a billion people speak Chinese instead. As the world becomes more connected, the need to remove language barriers is increasing.

The world is rapidly becoming more connected. More and more businesses are trying to break into foreign markets. As a result, tackling language **barriers** has become a primary concern. However, working with human translators can be slow and costly. To meet
5 the growing demand, software companies have released various translation **applications**.

There are numerous translation apps on the market. Some can be used to translate web content. This might include web pages, search engine results, and advertisements. Other apps can be used
10 on smartphones to translate things we see in everyday life. These apps can translate signs, **physical** documents, and language content in posters. As many of these applications **utilize** AI, they are capable of learning. Thus, the technology improves as people use it.

Translation software comes with numerous benefits. Firstly, the
15 applications are accessible, meaning anyone can download and use them. The applications work quickly, translating content within seconds. If the translation is needed urgently, the user will not need to wait for long. Secondly, the apps are convenient. They can be taken anywhere you can bring your smartphone.

20 Unfortunately, not all translation apps are equal. In some cases, a given app is great at translating a language like English. However, it may be terrible at translating Chinese. It is difficult for users to determine which apps are best for each language. This can lead to embarrassing **mistranslations**. Furthermore, many apps are incapable
25 of understanding certain aspects of a language. These could include cultural **elements** and words that have multiple meanings.

As the technology improves, however, many people believe these problems will be solved. Popular social media platforms are investing in translation software.
30 Likewise, numerous businesses are already relying on the software to communicate across languages. However, some companies do not fully trust app translations. Thus, they hire human translators to check the translations for errors.   Words 308

Q
What is the paragraph mainly about?

P1 Why _____ applications were developed

P2 What various translation applications can (do / make)

P3 The _____ of using translation applications

P4 The disadvantages of using translation _____

P5 The (future / end) of translation applications

CHECK YOUR COMPREHENSION

Choose the best answers.

Main idea   1   **What is the main idea of the passage?**

      a. Without AI, translation apps would not be possible.

      b. As technology improves, translation apps will no longer be needed.

      c. There are more disadvantages than benefits to using translation apps.

      d. Translation apps are being developed to bring down language barriers.

Details   2   **Translation apps can translate things _____ such as web pages, search engine results, and advertisements.**

      a. in the news

      b. on social media

      c. on the Internet

      d. on streets

   3   **Which is NOT a benefit of using translation apps?**

      a. They can translate content very quickly.

      b. They can be downloaded and used by anyone.

      c. They can translate all languages equally.

      d. They can be used anywhere on a smartphone.

   4   **According to the passage, which question CANNOT be answered?**

      a. What is difficult for users to determine?

      b. What type of content do the applications translate?

      c. Who is investing in translation software these days?

      d. How much does it cost to use translation applications?

Write the answers in complete sentences.

   5   **Which aspects of a language might be hard for a translation app to translate?**

_____

   6   **What do some companies do when they do not trust translation apps?**

_____

SHOW YOUR COMPREHENSION

Fill in the chart with the phrases from the box.

Translation Applications

What They Do	• translate web content and ❶_____
The Benefits	• are accessible, meaning everyone ❷_____ • convenient and ❸_____ you can bring your smartphone
The Disadvantages	• difficult to determine which apps are best for each language, which can ❹_____ • might not understand ❺_____ and words with multiple meanings

can download and use them	lead to embarrassing mistranslations
can be taken anywhere	things in everyday life	certain cultural elements

SUMMARIZE YOUR READING

Complete the summary with the words from the box.

benefits	demand	cultural	accessible
problems	web content	multiple	certain languages

To tackle language barriers, the ❶_____ for translation applications has grown. There are numerous translation apps on the market these days. They can be used to translate ❷_____ or things we see in everyday life. There are numerous ❸_____ when it comes to using translation apps. The apps are ❹_____, they work quickly, and they can be used wherever you take your smartphone. However, there are a few ❺_____ associated with translation apps. Some apps are great at translating ❻_____ but are bad at translating others. Additionally, they have trouble translating ❼_____ elements and words with ❽_____ meanings. In the future, however, these problems may be solved.

Which Form of Communication Is the Most Convenient?

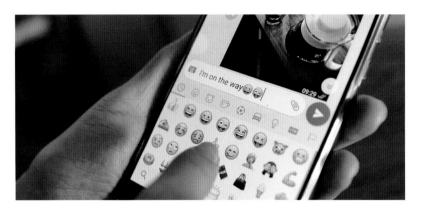

STEP 1 **DISCUSSION** **Talk to your partner and answer the questions.**

1. What do you normally use to communicate with your friends?

2. What are the benefits of using that form of communication?

STEP 2 **ORGANIZATION** **Fill in the chart with the phrases from the box.**

easy to use	a smartphone, tablet, or computer
a group chat feature	sending various types of content
families and study groups	let you send other forms of media

Introduction	The most convenient way to communicate is through instant messenger applications.
Body	**Supporting sentence 1:** Instant messenger apps are _____. **Details:** All you need is _____, and you can download and use the apps for free. **Supporting sentence 2:** In addition to sending messages, the apps also _____. **Details:** You can share photos, videos, and sound clips easily. **Supporting sentence 3:** The apps also have _____. **Details:** You can add multiple users to the group, which is convenient for _____.
Conclusion	Instant messenger applications are the most convenient way to communicate because they are easy to use, capable of _____, and have a group chat feature.

STEP 3 FIRST DRAFT   **Complete the writing with the phrases from the chart.**

Title Which Form of Communication is the Most Convenient?

The most convenient way to communicate is through instant messenger applications.

First, instant messenger apps are _____. All you need is _____, and you can download and use the apps for free.

Second, in addition to sending messages, the apps also _____ _____. You can share photos, videos, and sound clips easily.

Finally, the apps also have _____. You can add multiple users to the group, which is convenient for _____.

In conclusion, instant messenger applications are the most convenient way to communicate because they are easy to use, capable of _____ _____, and have a group chat feature.

STEP 4 FINAL DRAFT   **Complete the writing. Replace one of the details with your own idea.**

Title _____

The most convenient way to communicate is through instant messenger applications.

First, _____

_____

Second, _____

_____

Finally, _____

_____

In conclusion, instant messenger applications are the most convenient way to communicate because _____

_____

CHAPTER
02

THINK & WRITE 2

What Are Some Negative Effects of Urbanization?

Many Moons

WARM UP

1. How many moons do you think there are in the solar system?
2. Which planet do you think has the most moons?

BEFORE YOU READ

A   Match the words with the definitions below.

1. _____ orbit   a. rounded in shape

2. _____ equate   b. covered with bumps

3. _____ spherical   c. to crash into something

4. _____ lumpy   d. to make certain something exists or is true

5. _____ collide   e. to make a curved path around an object

6. _____ confirm   f. to consider two things to be the same

B   Background Knowledge

There are eight planets in our solar system. Mercury, Venus, Earth, and Mars are known as the inner planets. These planets are rocky and close to the sun. Jupiter, Saturn, Uranus, and Neptune are the outer planets. These planets are gas giants, which are much larger than the inner planets. Beyond them, there are dwarf planets, such as Pluto.

Moons are natural objects that **orbit** a planet or an asteroid. Although Earth only has one moon, there are over 200 moons in our solar system. Also known as natural satellites, moons generally are solid, and most do not have an atmosphere. However, moons

5 come in a wide variety of shapes and have different features.

There aren't many moons orbiting our solar system's inner planets. Mercury and Venus do not have any moons, and Mars only has two. Some of the outer planets, however, have numerous moons. Jupiter, for example, has 79 moons while Saturn has 82.

10 These planets likely have more moons because they are larger in size. A larger size **equates** to a larger gravitational field, which can better pull in objects.

Because Earth's moon is rounded, most people assume all moons are **spherical**. However, this is untrue as many moons are

15 **lumpy** and irregular in shape. Phobos and Deimos, Mars' two moons, are both examples of lumpy, oddly shaped moons. Some moons are similar to planets in that they have oceans and volcanoes. Europa, which orbits

20 Jupiter, is an ocean moon while Io, also orbiting Jupiter, is a volcanic moon. Similarly, Saturn has two moons that feature oceans, Enceladus and Titan.

◀ Phobos and Deimos

Scientists believe that most moons formed from the gas and

25 dust that were circling the sun after the formation of the solar system. However, some moons formed elsewhere and were caught by a planet's orbit. It is likely that Earth's moon formed about 4.5 billion years ago when a large body **collided** with Earth. The remaining debris collected to form the pale, rocky sphere we now

30 see in the night sky.

Although there are over 200 moons in the solar system, some of them are provisional moons. These are moons that may have been detected, but scientists have not been able to **confirm** their existence. Thus, as technology improves, scientists may find many more moons in our solar system. **Words 323**

Q

What is the paragraph mainly about?

P1 What _____ are

P2 The (types / number) of moons planets have

P3 The (shapes / locations) and features of moons

P4 How moons _____

P5 The future of _____ moons

CHECK YOUR COMPREHENSION

Choose the best answers.

<u>Main idea</u>   **1   What is the passage mainly about?**

    a. The differences between moons and planets

    b. How scientists detect and confirm moons

    c. When the moons in our solar system formed

    d. The moons in our solar system and their features

<u>Details</u>   **2   Which is true according to the passage?**

    a. Saturn currently has 79 moons in its orbit.

    b. Phobos and Deimos both look similar to Earth's moon.

    c. Earth's moon likely formed when two moons collided.

    d. Mars has two moons while Mercury doesn't have any.

3   Europa, Enceladus, and Titan are all moons that feature

    _____.

    a. atmospheres

    b. bodies of water

    c. volcanoes

    d. lumpy surfaces

4   Why do Jupiter and Saturn likely have more moons than other planets?

    a. They hit Earth about 4.5 billion years ago.

    b. They have more dust and gas circling them.

    c. Their gravitational fields can attract objects better.

    d. Their moons collide and break into smaller moons.

Write the answers in complete sentences.

5   What do scientists believe most moons formed from?

_____

6   What are provisional moons?

_____

SHOW YOUR COMPREHENSION

Fill in the chart with the phrases from the box.

Location	• not many moons ❶_____ • outer planets ❷_____ because they are larger in size
Features	• can be rounded or ❸_____ • some ❹_____ like planets do
Formation	• formed from gas and dust after the formation of the solar system • Earth's moon – likely formed when ❺_____

a large body collided with Earth   lumpy and irregular in shape
have oceans and volcanoes   have more moons   orbiting the inner planets

SUMMARIZE YOUR READING

Complete the summary with the words from the box.

confirmed   dust   Earth's moon   natural
rounded   numerous   pull objects   inner planets

Moons are ❶_____ satellites that orbit a planet or an asteroid. There are many types of moons with different features. The solar system's ❷_____ do not have many moons. In contrast, the outer planets have ❸_____ moons. This is likely due to their large size and ability to ❹_____ into orbit. Moons can be ❺_____ or lumpy, and some feature oceans and volcanoes. It is believed that most moons formed from ❻_____ and gas that circled the sun long ago. ❼_____ may have formed after a large object collided with the planet. Currently, some moons are considered provisional moons, meaning scientists haven't yet ❽_____ their existence.

Math in Our Everyday Lives

WARM UP

1. What is the most difficult math concept you have learned?
2. How often do you use math in your daily life?

BEFORE YOU READ

A   Match the words with the definitions below.

1. _____ whole (*n.*)   a. exact or accurate

2. _____ tedious   b. all of something

3. _____ figure out   c. boring and taking too long

4. _____ ingredient   d. to find an answer to something; to calculate

5. _____ precise   e. to find the size, length, or amount of something

6. _____ measure   f. one of the foods used to make a particular dish

B   Background Knowledge

Math is a part of so much of what we experience. It plays a role in our technology, our understanding of our planet, and even our understanding of time. It is impossible to determine who invented math as it dates back to prehistoric times. Early humans used simple math to make choices in their everyday lives.

It might not seem like it at times, but math is an important part of our daily lives. For example, people often use fractions and decimals, which are both related to math. A fraction is a part of a **whole**. One half and three-quarters are both fractions. A decimal is
5 simply a fraction changed into a number such as 0.5 or 0.75.

Many people find learning fractions to be **tedious**. But these concepts are responsible for much of what we experience. For example, when we drive a car with less than a full tank, we like to know how much is left. We use fractions like a half, a third, or
10 a quarter to determine how much is left and how far we can drive with that much gas.

Decimals are useful when we buy groceries. Imagine there are two different brands of milk being sold at different prices. One is 0.8 liters, and the other is 1.5 liters. Since we know the exact amount of
15 milk in each container, we can **figure out** which is cheaper to buy by changing the total price of the milk to the price per liter or milliliter.

When cooking at home, we use fractions and decimals as well.
20 Recipes list the amounts of the **ingredients** we need, and to be more **precise**, they use fractions and decimals.
25 For example, we might need one-third of a cup of flour or 2.5 tablespoons of sugar. So by using fractions and decimals, we can **measure** the exact amount of each ingredient.

As technology develops, some people claim it is not important to learn math. They say that their smartphones and other devices
30 have special applications that can do calculations. However, we should learn to rely on our minds to solve problems as we might not always have access to such technology. Thus, understanding math will make your life more convenient. Words 314

Q
What is the paragraph mainly about?

P1 What _____ and decimals are

P2 How we use (fractions / decimals) when driving

P3 How we use decimals when _____ shopping

P4 How _____ use fractions and decimals

P5 Why learning (math / smartphones) is important

CHECK YOUR COMPREHENSION

Choose the best answers.

Main idea **1 What is the passage mainly about?**

    a. The difficulty of learning math

    b. The importance of math in school

    c. How fractions and decimals have changed

    d. How fractions and decimals are used in our lives

Details **2 Which is mentioned as an example of using fractions and decimals?**

    a. To divide food into equal parts

    b. To determine the amount of fuel left in a gas tank

    c. To calculate the price of a discounted item

    d. To determine how much food is needed for a party

3 When you buy some milk, you can _____ by using decimals.

    a. choose high-quality milk

    b. get milk at a better price

    c. buy the exact amount of milk you need

    d. figure out how much milk you will drink in a week

4 What can be inferred from the passage?

    a. It takes a lot of time to learn fractions and decimals.

    b. Mathematics is not a practical subject in people's lives.

    c. Knowing fractions and decimals is important in the real world.

    d. People with calculators do not need to know fractions and decimals.

Write the answers in complete sentences.

5 How is a decimal related to a fraction?

_____

6 Why do some people claim it is not important to learn math?

_____

SHOW YOUR COMPREHENSION

Fill in the chart with the phrases from the box.

Fractions and Decimals	
Definitions	• fraction: ❶_____ • decimal: ❷_____
When Driving	• can determine how much gas is left in a tank • use fractions ❸_____
When Buying Groceries	• Different brands are sold at different prices. • can figure out which is ❹_____
When Cooking	• Recipes list ingredients in fractions and decimals. • ❺_____ using fractions and decimals

can measure the exact amount   a fraction changed into a number
a part of a whole   cheaper by using decimals   like a half, a third, and a quarter

SUMMARIZE YOUR READING

Complete the summary with the words from the box.

left   cheaper   a number   groceries
frequently   ingredients   determining   fraction

A ❶_____ is a part of a whole. A decimal is simply a fraction that is changed into ❷_____. Fractions and decimals are ❸_____ used in our lives. For instance, when we drive a car with less than a full tank of gas, we like to know the amount of fuel ❹_____ in the gas tank. We use the fractions a half, a third, and a quarter when ❺_____ this. In addition, when we buy ❻_____ such as milk, we can figure out which brand is ❼_____ to buy by using decimals. Even when we cook, we use fractions and decimals to measure the exact amount of the ❽_____ we need to use.

Subject Art & Music
Topic Disabled Artists

Having Difficulties?
No Problem!

WARM UP

1. What difficulties have you had to overcome?
2. When you have a problem, who helps you?

BEFORE YOU READ

A Match the words with the definitions below.

1. _____ encounter   a. poor and disadvantaged
2. _____ despair   b. a mental or physical illness
3. _____ spectacular   c. very impressive and dramatic
4. _____ deprived   d. a feeling that you have no hope at all
5. _____ disorder   e. the effort someone puts into something
6. _____ dedication   f. to experience something, especially a problem

B Background Knowledge

A disability is any difference or disorder that causes difficulties in a person's life. Many disabilities are visible physical differences. These disabilities can affect movement or a person's ability to breathe, eat, or sleep. Other disabilities are invisible in that they may affect a person's health or mental well-being, but we cannot see them.

People often **encounter** difficulties in their lives. These difficulties cause some people to fall into **despair** while they make others stronger. Some even have **spectacular** successes as they use their experiences as inspiration. Many popular artists, musicians, 5 and writers are remembered for the way they transformed their difficulties into beautiful creations.

Pablo Picasso was a Spanish painter born in 1881. During Picasso's Blue Period, he painted mostly in shades of blue and portrayed **deprived** people. At that time, he was suffering from 10 a severe case of depression. He was also living in poverty and having a hard time supporting himself. Instead of quitting painting, however, Picasso expressed his feelings through his art and created many unforgettable works, which eventually brought him fame.

Ray Charles, one of 15 the best-known American musicians, lost his ability to see when he was only six. However, his mother always said that he could do anything 20 just like everyone else. At the age of fifteen, he moved to Florida alone to study music. He eventually became famous and helped create a new genre of music called soul. Being blind never stopped Ray Charles from doing what he loved the most or from creating beautiful songs.

25 Korean musician, Heeah Lee, was born with a physical **disorder** that caused her to have two fingers on each hand and short legs. When she was a child, her mother had her play the piano to make her fingers stronger. Heeah's piano teacher thought it was impossible for her to play. Still, encouraged by her mother, Heeah 30 did not give up. In time, she learned to play the piano and even won numerous contests.

Their lives were not always easy, but Pablo Picasso, Ray Charles, and Heeah Lee did not give up. Instead, through hard work and **dedication**, they became accomplished in their fields. Their stories inspire many others to overcome their own difficulties.   Words 313

Q

What is the paragraph mainly about?

P1 How difficulties can (inspire / educate) people

P2 How Pablo Picasso overcame depression and _____

P3 How _____ overcame his difficulties and became famous

P4 How Heeah Lee overcame a physical _____

P5 The (impact / personalities) of Pablo Picasso, Ray Charles, and Heeah Lee

CHECK YOUR COMPREHENSION

Choose the best answers.

Main idea

1 **What is the passage mainly about?**

   a. How to become a great artist

   b. The importance of positive thinking

   c. Artists who overcame their difficulties

   d. Artists who have achieved worldwide fame

Details

2 **According to the passage, which is true about Pablo Picasso?**

   a. He suffered from depression all his life.

   b. He used only blue in all of his paintings.

   c. He quit painting so he could get a job.

   d. He shared his feelings in his artwork.

3 **According to the passage, which is NOT true about Ray Charles?**

   a. He was blind when he was born.

   b. He kept studying music thanks to his mother.

   c. He spent some time studying music in Florida.

   d. His songs are loved by many American people.

4 **Heeah Lee's problem was that** _____.

   a. she was not able to hear or see at all

   b. she had trouble learning how to read music

   c. she had shorter fingers and legs than most people

   d. she had fewer fingers than normal on both of her hands

Write the answers in complete sentences.

5 **What did Ray Charles help create?**

   _____

6 **Why did Heeah Lee start playing the piano?**

   _____

SHOW YOUR COMPREHENSION

Fill in the chart with the phrases from the box.

Artists Who Overcame Their Difficulties	
Pablo Picasso	• ❶_____ during his Blue Period • created great works of art by expressing his feelings ❷_____
Ray Charles	• became blind at the age of six • continued studying music and ❸_____
Heeah Lee	• ❹_____ on each hand and short legs • learned to play the piano and ❺_____

suffered from severe depression   was born with two fingers

won numerous contests   through his art   created beautiful songs

SUMMARIZE YOUR READING

Complete the summary with the words from the box.

overcome   difficulties   blind   inspiration

Blue Period   award-winning   musician   successful

Most people experience ❶_____ in life. Some fall into despair, but others

become stronger. Many artists use their difficulties as ❷_____. For instance,

Pablo Picasso created great works of art during his ❸_____, when he suffered

from severe depression. Ray Charles became ❹_____ when he was six, but he

kept studying music and became a famous American ❺_____. Korean Heeah

Lee, despite having only two fingers on each hand, became a(n) ❻_____

pianist. All three of these people became ❼_____ because they refused to

give up. To this day, they inspire others to ❽_____ their own problems.

UNIT 08 |

Subject History
Topic The Industrial Revolution

A Revolution That Changed the World

WARM UP

1. What types of jobs are the most common these days?
2. How are goods normally produced in modern society?

BEFORE YOU READ

A **Match the words with the definitions below.**

1. _____ transformation
2. _____ burst
3. _____ bring about
4. _____ facilitate
5. _____ intervention
6. _____ maximize

a. to cause; to lead to

b. a sudden increase; an explosion

c. to make something as large as possible

d. a complete change in form, appearance, or character

e. to make something easier or more likely to happen

f. the act of getting involved in a situation to change it

B **Background Knowledge**

Long ago, factories used wind or water to power their machines. This meant factories needed to be built close to rivers or windy areas. The invention of the steam engine changed all that. To operate a steam engine, water was heated with burning coal. The resulting steam could then power a variety of engines found in factories, ships, and even on trains.

Until the early 1700s, agriculture was the means of existence for most people in England. For generations, people made their living by farming and manufacturing, using hand tools and simple machines. But in the following 150 years, there was a great
5 **transformation** which changed England into an industrialized and urbanized country.

This period was called the Industrial Revolution. It took place in the 18th and 19th centuries. During this time, there was a **burst** of new ideas and new technological inventions. It **brought about** the
10 construction of roads, railways, and canals and, accordingly, great cities, factories, and mills. This change spread beyond England and resulted in the industrialization of other countries. But what made the revolution happen, and why did it start in England?

First of all, great deposits of coal contributed to England's role
15 as the birthplace of the Industrial Revolution. Coal was an essential fuel during industrialization. Increasing needs for the fuel led to the invention of the steam engine. This **facilitated** an abundant supply of cheap coal and sped up industrialization. The free expression of new ideas was another factor which greatly influenced the
20 revolution. More efficient steam engines were developed by inventors through the productive exchange of scientific ideas.

England also had the right political background for a *free-market system. Compared to other European powers, England did not have a strong monarchy. So the English people could pursue
25 their own objectives and earn money for themselves with very little government **intervention**. Finally, England's naval power significantly contributed to the spread of industrialization. The navy protected private traders, and this **maximized** overseas trade and profits.

30 The Industrial Revolution brought about many positive changes around the world. It greatly helped economies grow and gave average people job opportunities. However, there were many negative effects. These included dangerous work environments in factories, an increase in air pollution, and cramped, dirty living conditions as cities grew. Words 315

*__free-market system__ an economic system of buying and selling goods that is not controlled by a government

Q
What is the paragraph mainly about?
P1 How people lived _____ the Industrial Revolution

P2 What happened during the _____

P3 What (caused / stopped) the Industrial Revolution in England

▲ Steam engine

P4 How England's _____ background helped the revolution

P5 The _____ and negatives of the Industrial Revolution

CHECK YOUR COMPREHENSION

Choose the best answers.

Main idea **1** **What is the passage mainly about?**

a. Great inventions and their English inventors

b. The impact of the Industrial Revolution on Europe

c. The importance of natural resources on industrialization

d. Factors contributing to the Industrial Revolution in England

Details **2** **According to the passage, which is true?**

a. The Industrial Revolution occurred only in England.

b. Most English people were farmers before the 18th century.

c. Machines were not used before the Industrial Revolution.

d. There were few intelligent people in Europe in the 1800s.

3 **All of the following contributed to the Industrial Revolution EXCEPT**
_____ .

a. abundant coal deposits

b. the free exchange of ideas

c. the free-market system

d. an absolute monarchy

4 **Which is mentioned as a change that happened during the Industrial Revolution?**

a. Many new technological inventions appeared.

b. People manufactured goods with simple tools.

c. The price of coal rose because more people needed it.

d. The government prohibited individuals from trading overseas.

Write the answers in complete sentences.

5 **Why did the need for coal increase during the Industrial Revolution?**

_____

6 **How did the English navy contribute to the Industrial Revolution?**

_____

SHOW YOUR COMPREHENSION

Fill in the chart with the phrases from the box.

The Industrial Revolution in England	
Before the Revolution	• People lived by ❶_____, using simple tools and machines.
Contributors	• ❷_____ • the free expression of new ideas • the right political background ❸_____ • a powerful navy that protected private traders
Effects	• helped economies and ❹_____ • caused ❺_____, air pollution, and cramped living conditions

increased job opportunities   dangerous work environments

farming and manufacturing   for a free-market system   an abundant supply of coal

SUMMARIZE YOUR READING

Complete the summary with the words from the box.

benefited   political   transform   factors

industrialized   abundant   exchanged   influence

The Industrial Revolution occurred in England during the 18th and 19th centuries. The revolution had a great ❶_____ on the country, and it spread to other countries as well. Furthermore, it helped England ❷_____ into a wholly new country that was ❸_____ and urbanized. There were a lot of ❹_____ that led to the revolution. At that time, the supply of coal was ❺_____ in England, and new ideas were freely ❻_____. In addition, England had the right ❼_____ background for a free-market system, and it also had a strong navy that protected traders. The Industrial Revolution ❽_____ average people, but there were also several negative effects.

THINK & WRITE 2

 What Are Some Negative Effects of Urbanization?

STEP 1 **DISCUSSION** **Talk to your partner and answer the questions.**

1. Do you know of any urbanized regions? Can you give an example?

2. What characteristics does the region have?

STEP 2 **ORGANIZATION** **Fill in the chart with the phrases from the box.**

creates traffic problems   emissions from cars and factories

affects people negatively   the high cost of living in big cities

leaves some living in poverty   makes traffic congestion even worse

Introduction	Although urbanization has many positive effects on human life, there are several important problems with it.
Body	Supporting sentence 1: One negative effect is air pollution. Details: Nowadays, many countries are suffering from climate change, and _____ in cities are mainly responsible for it. Supporting sentence 2: _____ is another problem. Details: As more people move to cities, living expenses such as food and housing rapidly increase, which _____. Supporting sentence 3: Urbanization also _____ in most populated areas. Details: Many people drive their cars into downtown areas to get to work, and this _____.
Conclusion	Urbanization _____ because it pollutes the air, raises the cost of living, and causes heavy traffic.

FIRST DRAFT **Complete the writing with the phrases from the chart.**

Title What Are Some Negative Effects of Urbanization?

Although urbanization has many positive effects on human life, there are several important problems with it.

First, one negative effect is air pollution. Nowadays, many countries are suffering from climate change, and _____ in cities are mainly responsible for it.

Second, _____ is another problem. As more people move to cities, living expenses such as food and housing rapidly increase, which _____.

Lastly, urbanization also _____ in most populated areas. Many people drive their cars into downtown areas to get to work, and this _____.

In conclusion, urbanization _____ because it pollutes the air, raises the cost of living, and causes heavy traffic.

STEP 4 **FINAL DRAFT** **Complete the writing. Replace one of the details with your own idea.**

Title _____

Although urbanization has many positive effects on human life, there are several important problems with it.

First, _____

_____

Second, _____

_____

Lastly, _____

_____

In conclusion, urbanization _____

_____

CHAPTER
03

THINK & WRITE 3

Which Three Things in Your Country Would You Introduce to Tourists?

UNIT 09

Subject Life Science
Topic Typhoons

The Power of Nature

WARM UP

1. What was the most powerful storm you have ever witnessed?
2. In your opinion, what natural disasters are the most dangerous?

BEFORE YOU READ

A **Match the words with the definitions below.**

1. _____ landslide
2. _____ tropical
3. _____ accompany
4. _____ classify
5. _____ demolish
6. _____ last

a. to destroy completely
b. to continue to exist or happen
c. in or from the hottest parts of the world
d. to happen or occur with something else
e. to decide what group something belongs to
f. the falling of earth or rocks down a mountain or cliff

B **Background Knowledge**

Cyclones are large masses of air that rotate, often with powerful winds. In the Northern Hemisphere, they spin counterclockwise, but in the Southern Hemisphere, they rotate clockwise. Cyclones have different names depending on their locations. They might be called hurricanes, typhoons, tropical cyclones, or willy-willies.

On November 8, 2013, Typhoon Haiyan, also known as Typhoon Yolanda, hit the Philippines. Its powerful winds caused flooding and **landslides**, and nearly 10,000 people were killed or injured. It became the worst typhoon ever recorded to hit the country and
5 caused the greatest amount of destruction.

Q
What is the paragraph mainly about?
P1 The most destructive typhoon in the
_____

P2 How and (when / where) typhoons form

Like all typhoons, Typhoon Haiyan was a **tropical** storm that formed in the western
10 part of the North Pacific Ocean. Typhoons are **accompanied** by heavy rain and have very strong winds moving in a circular

▲ Destruction caused by Typhoon Haiyan

15 motion. The center of the storm is called the eye and is where the weather is usually calm. Many typhoons develop in areas of low air pressure over warm water. Once a typhoon forms, it tends to grow stronger over warm water and weaker over cold water.

A typhoon is categorized depending on the speed of its winds.
20 According to the international standard, a tropical storm with wind speeds of more than 118 km/h is a typhoon. The Hong Kong Observatory has further divided typhoons into three different classifications: typhoon, severe typhoon, and super typhoon. A severe typhoon has winds of at least 150 km/h, and a super
25 typhoon has winds of at least 190 km/h. By that standard, Typhoon Haiyan was **classified** as a super typhoon since it had winds of up to 275 km/h.

P3 The three typhoon

The faster the winds blow, the more damage a typhoon causes. Strong winds can **demolish** everything in their path. In addition,
30 typhoons produce high waves that can travel far inland and cause flooding when they hit land. They might also cause flooding due to heavy rainfall as was the case with Typhoon Maemi, which struck Korea on September 8, 2003. It was the most powerful typhoon ever recorded in Korea with wind speeds of up to 195 km/h. The effects of the typhoon **lasted** for days and caused severe damages.

P4 What typhoons

Words 308

CHECK YOUR COMPREHENSION

Choose the best answers.

Main idea 1 **What is the passage mainly about?**

    a. How typhoons are classified

    b. Ways to help typhoon victims

    c. The formation and types of typhoons

    d. How Typhoon Haiyan affected the Philippines

Details 2 **According to the passage, which is NOT true about typhoons?**

    a. They form in the western part of the North Pacific Ocean.

    b. They develop in areas where the air pressure is high.

    c. They usually strengthen over warmer water.

    d. Their winds travel over 118 kilometers per hour.

3 **Typhoons are divided into different categories according to**

    _____ .

    a. where they are formed

    b. how fast their winds are

    c. how much rain they produce

    d. how much damage they cause

4 **According to the Hong Kong Observatory standard, what kind of storm was Typhoon Maemi?**

    a. A tropical storm

    b. A typhoon

    c. A severe typhoon

    d. A super typhoon

Write the answers in complete sentences.

5 **What kinds of damage did Typhoon Haiyan cause in the Philippines?**

    _____

6 **What is the center of the storm called, and what is it like?**

    _____

SHOW YOUR COMPREHENSION

Fill in the chart with the phrases from the box.

Typhoons

Definition	• ❶_____ formed in the western part of the North Pacific Ocean • come with heavy rain, strong winds, and high waves • The weather is usually calm ❷_____.
Formation	• develop in ❸_____ over warm water • ❹_____ and weaker over cold water
Classification	• typhoon: has winds of more than 118 km/h • severe typhoon: has winds of at least 150 km/h • ❺_____: has winds of at least 190 km/h

in the eye of a typhoon	grow stronger over warm water
super typhoon	areas of low air pressure	tropical storms

SUMMARIZE YOUR READING

Complete the summary with the words from the box.

high waves	super typhoons	strengthen	their winds
accompanied by	severe	warm water	classifications

A typhoon is a tropical storm that forms in the western part of the North Pacific Ocean. Most typhoons develop in areas of low air pressure over ❶_____. They have strong winds and are ❷_____ heavy rain and ❸_____. In addition, they can ❹_____ if they move over warm water. Depending on the speed of ❺_____, they can be divided into three different ❻_____: typhoons, ❼_____ typhoons, and super typhoons. Typhoon Haiyan in 2013 and Typhoon Maemi in 2003 are both classified as ❽_____ as they had wind speeds of greater than 190 km/h.

UNIT 10 |

Subject Social Studies
Topic Fast Fashion

Fashionable Pollution

WARM UP

1. How often do you shop for new clothing?
2. Where do you normally get your new clothes from?

BEFORE YOU READ

A   Match the words with the definitions below.

1. _____ sewing machine
2. _____ mass-produce
3. _____ advent
4. _____ replicate
5. _____ precaution
6. _____ inhumane

a. the beginning of something
b. to make a copy of something
c. something done to ensure safety
d. a device used to make clothing
e. lacking humanity, often harsh or cruel
f. to produce goods in large amounts using machines

B   Background Knowledge

Although online shopping was invented in 1979, it did not become popular until the early 2000s. In 2001, the company Amazon launched its mobile online shopping service. By 2003, there were over 50 billion dollars in yearly US sales. Since then, many companies have had great success in launching their own online shopping platforms.

Prior to the 1800s, getting new clothing was much more difficult than it is today. In fact, most people had to prepare their own fabrics and make their own clothing. But the Industrial Revolution changed the way clothing was made. With the invention of the

5 **sewing machine**, clothing was much easier to produce.

Clothing remained mostly practical up until the 1970s. At this time, clothing retailers began adopting high fashion elements into their designs. They used cheap labor to **mass-produce** clothing quickly. They then sold these items at a low cost. Suddenly, average

10 people could afford to look like celebrities. This phenomenon became known as fast fashion.

With the **advent** of online shopping, fast fashion has grown in popularity. Nowadays, celebrities lead very public lives. Clothing companies pay careful attention to what they are wearing. Then,

15 they **replicate** certain items and sell them cheaply. But as trends change fast, customers often throw away the items soon after in order to make room for the next trend.

This makes the fashion industry one of the biggest polluters in the world. Because clothing items are produced so quickly, many

20 environmental **precautions** are ignored. Companies often use toxic dyes that pollute water. They also use cheap textiles like polyester which eventually break down and end up in the oceans. Even natural textiles made from cotton are a problem since growing cotton uses up water resources. It also adds large amounts of

25 pesticides to the environment.

Fast fashion also impacts animals when they consume polluted resources. Additionally, animals are used to create items that include leather and fur. Many are killed only for the garments to end up in a landfill when the trend changes a few months

30 later. Some companies advertise their products as fake fur. In reality, though, many companies are using real fur that was produced in **inhumane** conditions.   Words 308

Q
What is the paragraph mainly about?

P1 How _____
was made in the past

P2 How
_____
affected clothing
production

P3 How (high / fast)
fashion works today

P4 How fast
fashion affects the
_____

P5 The impact of
fast fashion on
_____

CHECK YOUR COMPREHENSION

Choose the best answers.

Main idea 1 **What is the main idea of the passage?**

   a. Online shopping has changed the way we buy clothing.

   b. The fashion industry has mostly stopped using animals for fur.

   c. Changes in clothing production have harmed the environment.

   d. High fashion trends are to blame for the creation of fast fashion.

Details 2 **Which is NOT true about clothing after the 1970s?**

   a. It was sold at a lower cost.

   b. It was mass-produced using cheap labor.

   c. It was influenced by trends in high fashion.

   d. It was mostly made in factories by hand.

3 **The low cost of fast fashion allows average people to**

   _____ .

   a. become celebrities

   b. replicate clothing

   c. buy more practical clothing

   d. look like famous people

4 **Which is NOT mentioned as an impact of fast fashion?**

   a. Animals lose their homes when factories are built.

   b. Toxic dyes and cheap textiles pollute water resources.

   c. Producing natural textiles adds pesticides to the environment.

   d. Animals are killed inhumanely in order to make fur and leather.

Write the answers in complete sentences.

5 **How did people get new clothing before the invention of the sewing machine?**

_____

6 **What do clothing companies do after paying attention to what celebrities wear?**

_____

SHOW YOUR COMPREHENSION

Fill in the chart with the phrases from the box.

Fast Fashion

Before the 1970s	• The sewing machine ❶_____. • Clothing remained practical until the 1970s.
After the Advent of Online Shopping	• Fast fashion ❷_____. • Companies replicate what celebrities wear using cheap labor. • People can follow trends and buy cheap clothing.
Impacts on the Environment and Animals	• Dyes, textiles, and pesticides ❸_____. • Animals are killed to ❹_____. • The items ❺_____ when trends change.

> make leather and fur items   made clothing easier to produce
> grew in popularity   end up in landfills   pollute water resources

SUMMARIZE YOUR READING

Complete the summary with the words from the box.

> online shopping   sewing machine   precautions   polluter
> difficult to do   trends change   high fashion   mass-produce

In the past, producing new clothing was ❶_____. However, with the advent of the ❷_____, it became much cheaper and faster to ❸_____ clothing. Clothing companies began adopting ❹_____ elements into their designs and selling the items cheaply. This became known as fast fashion. Fast fashion has grown in popularity thanks to ❺_____. Unfortunately, this has made the fashion industry a major ❻_____. To produce garments quickly, many environmental ❼_____ are ignored. As a result, water resources are used up and polluted. Additionally, animals are killed to make leather and fur. These garments then end up in landfills when ❽_____.

UNIT 11 | Subject History
Topic The Holocaust

Things That We Shouldn't Forget

WARM UP

1. In your opinion, what was the most horrible event in history?
2. Why is it important to learn about historical events?

▲ Concentration camp

BEFORE YOU READ

A **Match the words with the definitions below.**

1. _____ murder
2. _____ blame
3. _____ exclude
4. _____ chamber
5. _____ innocent
6. _____ memorial

a. not guilty of a crime
b. a room used for a particular purpose
c. the crime of killing someone deliberately
d. to prevent someone from taking part in an activity
e. a structure built to remind people of a famous person or event
f. to say that someone is responsible for something bad

B **Background Knowledge**

Antisemitism is prejudice and discrimination toward Jewish people. The term was made in 1879 to describe the hostility and hatred some people felt toward Jewish people. Antisemitism was widespread in Europe and North America prior to the Holocaust. Today, some Jewish people still experience this type of discrimination.

Born a Jewish German, Anne Frank fled to the Netherlands with her family when the Nazis gained

5 control over Germany. In her diary, she wrote about the feelings and experiences she had while in hiding. After being caught and sent to a concentration camp,

10 Anne died of an illness. Later, her father found her diary and had it published. Today, it is one of the most widely read books about the Holocaust.

The Holocaust was the mass **murder** of Jewish Europeans by the Nazis during World War II. Long before the war, movements

15 that viewed the Jewish people in a negative way had begun to form in Germany. Meanwhile, the Nazi Party was founded by Adolf Hitler and his associates. He **blamed** Jewish Germans for many of Germany's problems. As Hitler gained more power, many Germans began to agree with his hateful opinions.

20 At first, various laws were passed to **exclude** Jewish people from German society. As a result, they lost their social rights, jobs, and even businesses. Finally, they were sent to facilities known as concentration camps. There, they were forced to work hard with very little food. The Nazis tested drugs on some of them, and others

25 even underwent experimental surgical procedures. Eventually, the Nazis began murdering the captives. Some camps had gas **chambers** designed to kill people in large numbers. Nazi soldiers simply shot others. During the Holocaust, millions of **innocent** Jewish Europeans suffered and died due to the orders of Hitler and

30 the Nazi Party.

Nowadays, it is important to remember the Holocaust. Many books and films about the Holocaust have been released. There are **memorials** throughout Europe where concentration camps used to exist. In the United States, there is a museum on the Holocaust.

35 These efforts help to ensure that such a terrible event never happens again. Words 302

Q
What is the paragraph mainly about?
P1 Anne Frank and her
_____

P2 How Jewish people were (excluded / viewed) in Nazi Germany

P3 What happened during the
_____

P4 How the Holocaust is _____ today

CHECK YOUR COMPREHENSION

Choose the best answers.

Main idea **1** **What is the passage mainly about?**

    a. The causes and effects of the Holocaust

    b. Anne Frank's story during World War II

    c. Why many Germans hated Jewish Europeans

    d. Why people should read Anne Frank's diary

Details **2** **According to the passage, which is NOT true about Anne Frank?**

    a. She was a Jewish girl from Germany.

    b. She hid from the Nazis in the Netherlands.

    c. She died in a concentration camp.

    d. She wanted to publish her diary.

3 **Which is NOT something that the captives experienced in concentration camps?**

    a. Shooting each other

    b. Working hard with little food

    c. Being put into gas chambers

    d. Undergoing experimental surgeries

4 **What can be inferred from the passage?**

    a. The Holocaust also happened during World War I.

    b. Most of the victims of the Holocaust were young children.

    c. Jewish people were not treated equally in German society.

    d. Many films about the Holocaust were made by Jewish Germans.

Write the answers in complete sentences.

5 **What happened in Germany when Hitler gained more power?**

_____

6 **How does Europe remember the Holocaust nowadays?**

_____

SHOW YOUR COMPREHENSION

Fill in the chart with the phrases from the box.

The Holocaust	
What It Was	• the ❶_____ by the Nazis during World War II
Causes	• Hitler ❷_____ for many of Germany's problems. • Many Germans began to agree with ❸_____.
Effects	• Jewish Germans were ❹_____. • Jewish Europeans were sent to concentration camps and ❺_____. • Millions of innocent Jewish people were killed.

> excluded from German society   mass murder of Jewish Europeans
> experienced great suffering   his hateful ideas   blamed Jewish Germans

SUMMARIZE YOUR READING

Complete the summary with the words from the box.

> concentration   diary   memorials   were killed
> occur again   problems   hated   discriminated

In her ❶_____, Anne Frank wrote about the time she spent in hiding during the Holocaust. The Holocaust was the mass murder of Jewish Europeans during World War II. Adolf Hitler ❷_____ the Jewish people. After his rise to power, many Germans began to believe that Germany's ❸_____ had been caused by Jewish Germans. During that time, Jewish people were ❹_____ against by German society. Later, they were sent to ❺_____ camps, where they experienced great suffering. Eventually, a large number of innocent Jewish people ❻_____. Nowadays, many books, films, ❼_____, and museums help people remember that such an event should never ❽_____.

Shared Treasures

WARM UP
1. What cultural sites have you visited?
2. What famous natural site do you want to see?

▲ The Great Temple of Abu Simbel

BEFORE YOU READ

A   Match the words with the definitions below.

1. _____ safeguard   a. at a very high risk of no longer existing

2. _____ relocate   b. the destroyed parts of a building or town

3. _____ establishment   c. to protect something from being harmed

4. _____ ruins   d. the act of starting an organization or system

5. _____ geological   e. relating to the features of the Earth's surface

6. _____ endangered   f. to move someone or something to a different place

B   Background Knowledge

The United Nations Educational, Scientific, and Cultural Organization (UNESCO) was formed in 1945, the same year WWII ended. After two terrible world wars, the founders of UNESCO believed that politics and economics could not bring about world peace. Rather, the world needed to share education, culture, and science in order to achieve peace.

The United Nations Educational, Scientific, and Cultural Organization (UNESCO) is a specialized agency of the United Nations. The main goal of UNESCO is to help improve worldwide peace and security by encouraging the world to cooperate through
5　education, science, and culture.

Believing that culture plays a role in human development, UNESCO has worked hard to protect World Heritage Sites. These heritage sites have a special cultural or physical significance to humankind. UNESCO believes they belong to all of us rather than
10　to any one nation, so they should be saved for future generations.

UNESCO's early efforts to **safeguard** the world's heritage include the Nubia Campaign in 1960. Egypt planned to construct a dam on the Nile River. However, the dam would have flooded an important site from ancient Egyptian civilization. The purpose of the campaign
15　was to **relocate** the Great Temple of Abu Simbel to a higher place. Thanks to the success of the effort, a series of similar campaigns led to the **establishment** of the UNESCO World Heritage Committee in 1976.

Since 1976, the UNESCO World Heritage Committee has
20　protected many sites. The sites are categorized as follows: cultural, natural, and mixed heritage. Cultural heritage includes monuments, ancient **ruins**, and buildings of universal value while natural heritage sites are selected for their natural value, including geographical and **geological** features. The last type is mixed
25　heritage, which includes sites with both cultural and natural value.

The UNESCO World Heritage list includes many famous locations, such as Australia's Great Barrier Reef and the Taj Mahal in India. Like many countries,
30　South Korea has numerous cultural heritage sites registered on the list.

◀ Great Barrier Reef

There is also an important natural heritage site, the Jeju Volcanic Island and Lava Tubes. It became a natural heritage site in 2007 and boasts an extraordinary volcanic landscape. It is also important geologically and is home to many **endangered** species.　Words 311

Q
What is the paragraph mainly about?

P1▶ What UNESCO is and its _____

P2▶ What UNESCO works hard to (disrupt / save), and why

P3▶ How the UNESCO World Heritage Committee was (relocated / formed)

P4▶ The (types / locations) of World Heritage Sites

P5▶ World Heritage Sites in _____ and around the world

CHECK YOUR COMPREHENSION

Choose the best answers.

Main idea 1 **What is the passage mainly about?**

a. The original founders of UNESCO

b. A list of World Heritage Sites around the world

c. The importance of preserving World Heritage Sites

d. The establishment of UNESCO and the types of World Heritage Sites

Details 2 **What was the purpose of the Nubia Campaign in 1960?**

a. To construct a dam on the Nile River

b. To move the Abu Simbel temple to a higher place

c. To establish the UNESCO World Heritage Committee

d. To include meaningful places on World Heritage List

3 **Natural heritage sites are chosen for their _____.**

a. political value

b. geological features

c. cultural importance

d. international fame

4 **Which is NOT true about World Heritage Sites?**

a. World Heritage Sites are divided into two types.

b. There are no buildings on the natural heritage list.

c. The Taj Mahal is a famous World Heritage Site in India.

d. South Korea has more than one cultural heritage site on the list.

Write the answers in complete sentences.

5 **Why does UNESCO believe World Heritage Sites should be saved for future generations?**

_____

6 **When and why did the Jeju Volcanic Island and Lava Tubes become a natural heritage site?**

_____

SHOW YOUR COMPREHENSION

Fill in the chart with the phrases from the box.

UNESCO World Heritage Sites	
Nubia Campaign	• saved the Abu Simbel temple from ❶_____
Types of World Heritage Sites	• cultural heritage: monuments, ❷_____ • natural heritage: sites with ❸_____ • mixed heritage: sites that have the features of both ❹_____
Examples of World Heritage Sites	• the Great Barrier Reef in Australia and the Taj Mahal in India • the Jeju Volcanic Island and Lava Tubes: extraordinary ❺_____ in South Korea

geographical and geological features   being flooded by the Nile River

natural heritage site   ancient ruins, and buildings   cultural and natural heritage

SUMMARIZE YOUR READING

Complete the summary with the words from the box.

mixed   saved   protects   universal value

promotes   cooperation   registered as   establishment

UNESCO ❶_____ world peace and security through global ❷_____

in education, science, and culture. In the area of culture, the organization reviews

and ❸_____ World Heritage Sites, which are places with ❹_____.

UNESCO's early work started with the Nubia Campaign. The campaign successfully

❺_____ an important site from ancient Egypt from being flooded by the Nile

River. Since the ❻_____ of the UNESCO World Heritage Committee in 1976,

meaningful sites have been ❼_____ cultural, natural, and ❽_____

heritage. Like most places, South Korea has many World Heritage Sites including the

Jeju Volcanic Island and Lava Tubes.

THINK & WRITE 3

Q **Which Three Things in Your Country Would You Introduce to Tourists?**

STEP 1 **DISCUSSION** **Talk to your partner and answer the questions.**

1. What is one thing your country is known for internationally?

2. What is one famous architectural site in your country?

STEP 2 **ORGANIZATION** **Fill in the chart with the phrases from the box.**

a wide variety of shows	see the country's amazing wildlife
many unique animals	another famous tourist location
tourists who love beaches	great for surfers and swimmers

Introduction	Australia has many interesting attractions, but I think tourists would be most interested in the following three.
Body	**Supporting sentence 1:** Many tourists visit Australia to _____ _____ . **Details:** Australia has _____ such as kangaroos, koalas, and wombats. **Supporting sentence 2:** The Sydney Opera House is _____ _____ . **Details:** The opera house offers tours and _____ . **Supporting sentence 3:** _____ will have a great time at Byron Bay. **Details:** This beach is _____ alike.
Conclusion	Australia has many exciting things, but the things sure to please visitors are the unique wildlife, the Sydney Opera House, and Byron Bay.

STEP 3 `FIRST DRAFT` **Complete the writing with the phrases from the chart.**

Title Which Three Things in Your Country Would You Introduce to Tourists?

Australia has many interesting attractions, but I think tourists would be most interested in the following three.

First, many tourists visit Australia to _____. Australia has _____ such as kangaroos, koalas, and wombats.

Second, the Sydney Opera House is _____. The opera house offers tours and _____.

Finally, _____ will have a great time at Byron Bay. This beach is _____ alike.

In conclusion, Australia has many exciting things, but the things sure to please visitors are the unique wildlife, the Sydney Opera House, and Byron Bay.

STEP 4 `FINAL DRAFT` **Complete the writing. Replace one of the details with your own idea.**

Title _____

Australia has many interesting attractions, but I think tourists would be most interested in the following three.

First, _____

_____

Second, _____

_____

Finally, _____

_____

In conclusion, Australia has many exciting things, but the things sure to please visitors are _____

_____

CHAPTER
04

THINK & WRITE 4

What Technology Do You Think Is Helpful for Learning?

UNIT 13 |

Subject Social Studies
Topic Eating Disorders

Body Image and Food

WARM UP

1. Have you ever felt like you needed to go on a diet?
2. What physical traits are considered beautiful in your country?

BEFORE YOU READ

A   Match the words with the definitions below.

1. _____ disordered   a. unable to be achieved
2. _____ avoidance   b. the act of taking something in
3. _____ intake   c. to get rid of something quickly
4. _____ flush   d. being done in a way that is not normal
5. _____ obesity   e. the state of being extremely overweight
6. _____ unattainable   f. the state of staying away from something

B   Background Knowledge

Throughout history beauty standards have changed dramatically. In Ancient Egypt, the ideal woman was slim while women in Ancient Greece were considered beautiful if they were chubbier. Nowadays, as fashion trends change more rapidly, so do beauty standards. Many people feel these standards are unattainable and could be responsible for eating disorders.

Eating disorders are serious mental health conditions. People who have eating disorders have an unhealthy relationship with food. Their thoughts about food might lead to **disordered** eating. This means they might eat too much food, or they might not eat
5 enough. What are the three main types of eating disorder?

Anorexia nervosa is a common eating disorder. People suffering from anorexia nervosa often believe they are overweight regardless of how much they actually weigh. This leads to food **avoidance** in which they refuse to eat certain foods. They might also restrict food
10 **intake** or only eat small portions of foods they deem safe. This in turn causes them to become dangerously underweight and may even result in death.

Similarly, bulimia nervosa is caused by the disordered belief that food intake should be restricted. However, instead of limiting
15 food intake, people who suffer from bulimia nervosa may go through periods where they eat large amounts of food. They then purge, which means they force themselves to vomit. They might also use medicines to quickly **flush** the food from their bodies.

Finally, binge eating is another common eating disorder. Rather
20 than restrict food intake, people with binge eating disorder suffer from periods of overeating. They often eat when they are not hungry, or they continue eating even after they are full. This often leads to weight gain and can develop into **obesity** if the sufferer does not receive treatment.

25 It is unclear what causes eating disorders. However, psychologists believe it could be several biological and social factors. Both men and women can suffer from eating disorders, but teen girls and young adult women are most at risk. Some experts point to the way young women
30 are portrayed in the media as a possible cause. Young girls often feel pressured by **unattainable** beauty standards. Thus, they develop unhealthy relationships with food.

Words 308

Q
What is the paragraph mainly about?

P1 What
_____ are

P2 What anorexia nervosa (is / works)

P3 What
_____ is

P4 (How / What) binge eating disorder is

P5 The possible
_____
of eating disorders

CHECK YOUR COMPREHENSION

Choose the best answers.

<u>Main idea</u> 1 **What is the passage mainly about?**

    a. Types of eating disorders and their causes

    b. Why people suffer from eating disorders

    c. The best cures for various eating disorders

    d. How an eating disorder affects a person's health

<u>Details</u> 2 **According to paragraph 2, which is NOT true about anorexia nervosa?**

    a. It causes people to feel as though they are overweight.

    b. It causes people to avoid food or restrict food intake.

    c. People who suffer from it might eat too much at times.

    d. People who suffer from it can die from being underweight.

3 **When people with bulimia nervosa purge, they attempt to**

    _____.

    a. overeat

    b. restrict food intake

    c. remove foods they ate

    d. weigh themselves

4 **What can be inferred from the passage?**

    a. Anorexia nervosa is the most common eating disorder.

    b. People with binge eating disorder do not usually feel hungry.

    c. Binge eating disorder is much more dangerous than bulimia nervosa.

    d. There may be multiple reasons why people develop eating disorders.

Write the answers in complete sentences.

5 **According to paragraph 1, what problem do people with eating disorders have?**

    _____

6 **Who commonly suffers from eating disorders?**

    _____

SHOW YOUR COMPREHENSION

Fill in the chart with the phrases from the box.

Eating Disorders	
Anorexia Nervosa	• Sufferers believe they are overweight. • This leads to ❶_____.
Bulimia Nervosa	• caused by the belief that ❷_____ • Sufferers commonly eat large amounts of food, then ❸_____.
Binge Eating Disorder	• Sufferers go through periods of overeating. • This can lead to ❹_____.
The Causes	• could be caused by several ❺_____

> food avoidance and weight loss biological and social factors
> purge by vomiting food should be restricted weight gain and obesity

SUMMARIZE YOUR READING

Complete the summary with the words from the box.

> be restricted unclear unhealthy obesity
> overweight unattainable overeat weight loss

People who have eating disorders have a(n) ❶_____ relationship with food.
People who have anorexia nervosa believe they are ❷_____. This leads to
food restriction and ❸_____. Likewise, bulimia nervosa is caused by the belief
that food needs to ❹_____. People with this disorder ❺_____, then
purge the food from their bodies. Alternatively, binge eating disorder causes people
to overeat frequently. This can lead to weight gain and ❻_____. The cause of
each disorder is ❼_____, but some experts point to the way ❽_____
beauty standards are portrayed in the media.

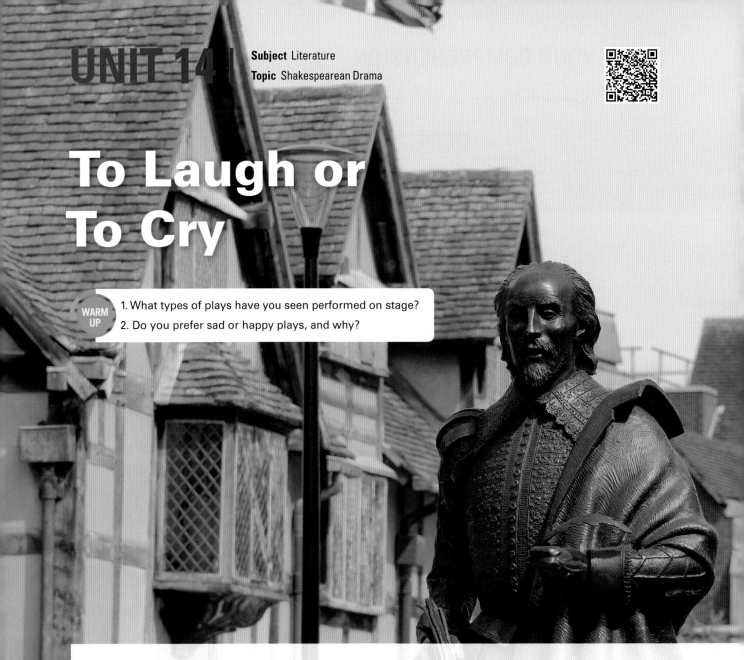

UNIT 14

Subject Literature
Topic Shakespearean Drama

To Laugh or To Cry

WARM UP

1. What types of plays have you seen performed on stage?
2. Do you prefer sad or happy plays, and why?

BEFORE YOU READ

A **Match the words with the definitions below.**

1. _____ playwright

2. _____ twist

3. _____ nobility

4. _____ tragic

5. _____ supernatural

6. _____ critic

a. very sad, often related to a death

b. a person who writes plays

c. a sudden and unexpected change in a story

d. people of a high social rank in a society

e. a person who judges a work of art or performance

f. things beyond scientific explanation, such as ghosts

B **Background Knowledge**

William Shakespeare lived between 1564 and 1616. Although not much is known about his personal life, historians believe he married at age 18 and had three children. Some time around the late 1580s, Shakespeare went to London to begin a new career. There, he worked as an actor, a writer, and became the co-owner of an acting company.

William Shakespeare was born in England in 1564. During his career as a **playwright**, he wrote 39 plays and 154 *sonnets. To this day, his plays are still studied and performed all around the world. They can be classified into three main types: comedies, tragedies, and tragicomedies.

Shakespeare's first plays were comedies. The term comedy does not have the same meaning it does today. In fact, many of Shakespeare's comedies were not humorous at all. Rather, the term refers to plays that have a happy ending. Usually, this involves
10 a marriage or a couple reuniting. The characters in comedies are often lower or middleclass people, and the plots are complex with many surprising **twists** and turns. *The Taming of the Shrew*, *A Midsummer Night's Dream*, and *Much Ado About Nothing* are all famous Shakespearean comedies.

15 Shakespeare wrote his tragedies later in life. Unlike his comedies, Shakespeare's tragedies usually feature **nobility** and royalty, and the
20 main character is usually considered a **tragic** hero. This means the hero has

▲Hamlet

some sort of flaw that ends up causing his or her death. Thus, tragedies always end sadly with the death of the hero. Furthermore,
25 Shakespeare's tragedies focus on more serious subject matter, such as revenge, the **supernatural**, and the difference between good and evil. *Othello*, *Romeo and Juliet*, *Hamlet*, and *Macbeth* are among the most popular of Shakespeare's tragedies.

Prior to his death, Shakespeare began to write tragicomedies.
30 Tragicomedies are neither tragedies nor comedies. Rather, they have features of both. For example, the main character may seem like a tragic hero only for the story to have a happy ending. **Critics** do not always agree on what can be considered a tragicomedy. But some suggest that *The Merchant of Venice* and *The Winter's Tale* are not comedies but tragicomedies. Words 296

***sonnet** a type of Italian poetry that includes 14 lines

Q

What is the paragraph mainly about?

P1 William Shakespeare and his life's (hardship / work)

P2 The features of Shakespeare's

P3 The features of Shakespeare's (tragedies / tragicomedies)

P4 What makes a

CHECK YOUR COMPREHENSION

Choose the best answers.

Main idea **1** **What is the passage mainly about?**

    a. How critics judge tragedies and comedies

    b. Types of Shakespearean plays and their features

    c. The life and death of a great English playwright

    d. The differences between tragedies and comedies

Details **2** **According to the passage, which is true about Shakespeare's comedies?**

    a. They focus on the death of the hero.

    b. They have complex but surprising plots.

    c. They feature royals as main characters.

    d. They seem tragic but have happy endings.

3 **Shakespeare's *Othello, Romeo and Juliet, Hamlet,* and *Macbeth* all have**
_____.

    a. a tragic hero

    b. a couple reuniting

    c. a happy ending

    d. lower class characters

4 **Why does the author mention *The Merchant of Venice* and *The Winter's Tale*?**

    a. To explain how Shakespeare's comedies differ from his tragedies

    b. To recommend two plays that end with the death of the main character

    c. To illustrate the differences between two of Shakespeare's tragicomedies

    d. To give examples of what some critics consider to be tragicomedies

Write the answers in complete sentences.

5 **How many plays and sonnets did Shakespeare write?**

_____

6 **What do Shakespeare's tragedies focus on?**

_____

SHOW YOUR COMPREHENSION

Fill in the chart with the phrases from the box.

Shakespeare's Plays	
Comedies	• plays that ❶_____, usually involving a marriage • featuring ❷_____ and complex plots
Tragedies	• feature ❸_____ and have a tragic hero • focus on revenge, the supernatural, and ❹_____ _____
Tragicomedies	• have features of ❺_____

both comedies and tragedies   the difference between good and evil
have a happy ending   nobility and royalty   lower or middleclass characters

SUMMARIZE YOUR READING

Complete the summary with the words from the box.

death   tragic   classified   critics
tragic hero   happy ending   tragicomedies   ending

During his career, Shakespeare wrote 39 plays. Each can be ❶_____ as one of the following: comedy, tragedy, or tragicomedy. Shakespeare wrote his comedies first. Comedies are plays that have a ❷_____, often featuring lower or middleclass characters. On the other hand, Shakespeare's tragedies usually feature nobility and royalty. They also have a ❸_____ ending, usually involving the ❹_____ of the hero. Later in life, Shakespeare wrote what are known as ❺_____. These plays have features common to both comedies and tragedies. For example, they might feature a ❻_____, but the ❼_____ might be happy. However, ❽_____ don't always agree on what makes a tragicomedy.

UNIT 15 |

Subject Social Studies
Topic Leadership

This Time, I Am the Leader!

WARM UP

1. Have you ever had to be a leader? Describe the situation.
2. Which world leader do you admire most?

BEFORE YOU READ

A **Match the words with the definitions below.**

1. _____ value (v.)
2. _____ morale
3. _____ coercive
4. _____ compliance
5. _____ reward
6. _____ penalty

a. a punishment for breaking a rule or law
b. something that is given for doing well
c. a level of confidence and cheerfulness
d. to think that someone or something is important
e. the practice of obeying a law, rule, or request
f. using force or threats to make someone do something

B **Background Knowledge**

Leaders are people who ensure an organization runs properly and reaches its goals. They do this by determining a set of goals, mapping out a path toward each goal, and inspiring others to put in the necessary work. Most leaders, such as presidents, prime ministers, CEOs, and business owners, have dynamic personalities and can easily inspire others.

What makes a great leader? Some believe certain people were born with the skills needed to become compelling leaders. Others believe people can learn to become leaders as they mature. However, there is more than one type of leader, and some leaders
5   might only be suited for one style. Additionally, some leadership styles are only useful in certain situations.

The democratic leadership style **values** the participation of team members while the leader still takes responsibility for the final decision. This type of leadership boosts the members' **morale** since
10 they can make their voices heard in the decision-making process. It makes them feel as if their opinions matter. Democratic leadership works well during times of change within an organization. However, it is not an ideal choice when an organization needs to make a quick decision or when the team members are not informed enough to
15 offer the leader suggestions.

Next, **coercive** leaders force their team members to follow their orders by threatening them with punishment. Instead of persuading people, these leaders demand immediate **compliance** with all of their orders. Coercive leadership is highly effective in short-
20 term and emergency situations when fast decisions are needed to prevent further chaos. However, leaders should rely on it only after everything else has failed. Otherwise, it can cause serious problems for an organization by hurting its flexibility.

Lastly, transactional leadership focuses on giving **rewards** and
25 punishments. After determining their goals together, the members agree to follow their leaders' directions to accomplish them. The leaders then either reward or punish the team members based upon the results of their performance. This method works when the rewards and punishments are what motivate the people involved.
30 However, it may cause people to get used to doing only what they are told to do. As a result, they might do the minimum amount of work expected of them to avoid **penalties**.   Words 312

Q

What is the paragraph mainly about?

P1 What makes a great
_____

P2 How the
_____
leadership style works

P3 How the
_____
leadership style works

P4 How the
_____
leadership style works

CHECK YOUR COMPREHENSION

Choose the best answers.

Main idea 1 **What is the passage mainly about?**

    a. How to motivate team members

    b. The special qualities that make a great leader

    c. Rewards and punishments that motivate people

    d. Different leadership styles for different situations

Details 2 **According to the passage, which is NOT true about democratic leadership?**

    a. It is not effective when time is limited.

    b. Team members participate in the decision-making process.

    c. All team members share responsibility for the final decision.

    d. It works well when there is an organizational change.

3 **What do coercive leaders use to make their team members follow orders?**

    a. Good listening skills

    b. Rewards for good work

    c. The threat of punishment

    d. The promise of a small workload

4 **What can be inferred about transactional leadership?**

    a. It provides more penalties than rewards.

    b. Team members are forced to do what they are told.

    c. The types of rewards are suggested by the members.

    d. Team members may not do their best when they work.

Write the answers in complete sentences.

5 **When is coercive leadership highly effective?**

_____

6 **When does transactional leadership work?**

_____

SHOW YOUR COMPREHENSION

Fill in the chart with the phrases from the box.

Types of Leadership	
Democratic Leadership	• based on the participation of team members • effective during ❶_____ • ineffective ❷_____
Coercive Leadership	• based on ❸_____ • effective during times of emergency • may hurt ❹_____
Transactional Leadership	• based on rewards and punishments • effective when team members are motivated • Team members may get used to ❺_____.

times of change in an organization	orders and immediate compliance
meeting minimum expectations	an organization's flexibility	when time is limited

SUMMARIZE YOUR READING

Complete the summary with the words from the box.

quick decision	compliance	motivate	punishment
participation	rewards	certain situations	an emergency

There are a few types of leadership. Each leadership style is useful in ❶_____.
First, democratic leaders encourage ❷_____ from their team members. While
this type of leadership is effective during times of change within an organization, it may
delay a ❸_____. Coercive leaders demand immediate ❹_____ with
their orders by threatening team members with ❺_____. While this works best
in ❻_____, it can hurt the flexibility of an organization. Lastly, transactional
leaders use ❼_____ and penalties. The method works when the rewards
and penalties are the things that ❽_____ the people involved. However, the
workers often only meet the minimum expectations.

UNIT 16

Subject Science
Topic Smart Textiles

Wear SMART!

WARM UP

1. What do you think the clothing of the future will look like?
2. Do you think clothing will be more expensive in the future?

180 pts

BEFORE YOU READ

A Match the words with the definitions below.

1. _____ textile	a. to change
2. _____ embed	b. woven or knitted cloth
3. _____ alter	c. the practical use or purpose of something
4. _____ function	d. to put something firmly into something else
5. _____ vitals	e. a substance, often dangerous to humans
6. _____ chemical (n.)	f. the organs that are needed to keep a person alive

B Background Knowledge

A textile is a material that is made by weaving threads into a fabric. Traditionally, textiles were made from natural materials such as silk or cotton. Smart textiles can be made from either natural materials or synthetic ones. Depending on the function of the smart textile, various electronic components are woven into the fabric.

People often wonder what the clothing of the future is going to be like. They imagine all sorts of styles that people might wear. The clothes of the future are going to be different in appearance and style, and they are also going to be different in one more important
5 way: most clothes in the future will be made of smart **textiles**.

Smart textiles are already used in some types of clothing. They are fabrics that have electronic materials, such as computer chips, **embedded** in them.
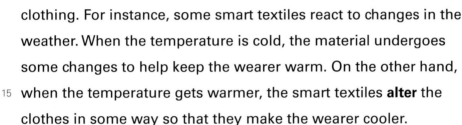
10 These electronics allow clothes made of smart textiles to be more than just clothing. For instance, some smart textiles react to changes in the weather. When the temperature is cold, the material undergoes some changes to help keep the wearer warm. On the other hand,
15 when the temperature gets warmer, the smart textiles **alter** the clothes in some way so that they make the wearer cooler.

Some smart textiles also have medical **functions**, which make them extremely important to certain people. Some individuals have medical conditions, such as heart problems, that require doctors
20 to constantly monitor them. Smart textiles have digital sensors in the fabric that can monitor blood sugar levels, blood pressure, and heart rate. If patients wear clothes made of smart textiles, they will not need doctors all the time because their clothes will monitor their **vitals**. If they are about to experience any problems, the
25 clothes will warn the wearers.

Smart textiles are used to make military uniforms as well. These uniforms protect soldiers from heat, dangerous **chemicals**, and gases. They also allow higher-ranking officers to monitor the health of each soldier. If a soldier gets wounded or sick, the uniform
30 makes it easier to stabilize him or her. As smart textiles continue to improve, they will likely have many more applications in the future.

Words 304

Q
What is the paragraph mainly about?

P1 What the _____ of the future will be like

P2 (How / When) smart textiles work

P3 How smart textiles help people with _____ problems

P4 How smart textiles are used in the _____

CHECK YOUR COMPREHENSION

Choose the best answers.

Main idea   1   **What is the passage mainly about?**

     a. The history of clothing and textiles

     b. Smart textiles and their medical uses

     c. How smart textiles can benefit our lives

     d. What smart textiles are made of

Details   2   **Clothes made of smart textiles can** _____ .

     a. tell the wearer the temperature

     b. keep the wearer warm or cool

     c. allow the wearer to access the Internet

     d. make the wearer feel lighter than he or she is

3   **According to the passage, how do medical patients benefit by wearing smart textiles?**

     a. Their clothes cure their diseases.

     b. Their clothes improve their health.

     c. Their clothes let them know their health status.

     d. Their clothes call their doctors if they have a problem.

4   **Which is true about smart textiles?**

     a. They are made of entirely new materials.

     b. They are not yet available for people to wear.

     c. They are too expensive for most people to buy.

     d. They currently have medical and military applications.

Write the answers in complete sentences.

5   **What are smart textiles?**

_____

6   **What do military uniforms made of smart textiles protect soldiers from?**

_____

SHOW YOUR COMPREHENSION

Fill in the chart with the phrases from the box.

Smart Textiles

How They Work	• fabrics that have electronic materials embedded in them • can ❶_____
Medical Uses	• ❷_____ that can monitor blood sugar levels, blood pressure, and heart rate • ❸_____ and warn of problems
Military Uses	• allow higher-ranking officers to ❹_____ • make it easier to ❺_____

can monitor a patient's vitals   react to weather changes

monitor the health of soldiers   stabilize the wounded   have digital sensors

SUMMARIZE YOUR READING

Complete the summary with the words from the box.

health status   protect   made of   electronic

react to   embedded in   uniforms   medical

In the future, clothing will be different in style, and most will be ❶_____ smart textiles. Already, some clothes are made of smart textiles, which are fabrics that have ❷_____ equipment ❸_____ them. These clothes can ❹_____ weather changes by keeping their wearers warm or cool. Clothes made of smart textiles are also used for ❺_____ purposes because they can constantly check the ❻_____ of a patient. In addition, some soldiers wear ❼_____ made of smart textiles. These uniforms help ❽_____ soldiers and treat those who get wounded.

THINK & WRITE 4

 What Technology Do You Think Is Helpful for Learning?

STEP 1 `DISCUSSION` **Talk to your partner and answer the questions.**

1. How often do you use the Internet for learning?

2. What kinds of technology do you see in your classroom?

STEP 2 `ORGANIZATION` **Fill in the chart with the phrases from the box.**

saves time and energy   makes studying more interesting

typing key words or phrases   can be more motivated to learn

have to go to a particular place   get information quickly and conveniently

Introduction	I think the Internet is helpful for learning in several ways.
Body	Supporting sentence 1: The Internet allows us to _____ _____. Details: Simply by _____ into a search engine, we can get the information we need in just a few seconds. Supporting sentence 2: Learning through the Internet _____ _____. Details: There are many lectures online. This means we do not _____ to attend a lecture. Supporting sentence 3: The Internet _____. Details: Compared to books, the Internet is more interactive and fun. So students _____.
Conclusion	The Internet helps us find information easily, lets us study at home, and motivates us to study more.

STEP 3 `FIRST DRAFT` **Complete the writing with the phrases from the chart.**

Title What Technology Do You Think Is Helpful for Learning?

I think the Internet is helpful for learning in several ways.

First, the Internet allows us to _____. Simply by _____ into a search engine, we can get the information we need in just a few seconds.

Second, learning through the Internet _____. There are many lectures online. This means we do not _____ to attend a lecture.

Lastly, the Internet _____. Compared to books, the Internet is more interactive and fun. So students _____.

In short, the Internet helps us find information easily, lets us study at home, and motivates us to study more.

STEP 4 `FINAL DRAFT` **Complete the writing. Replace one of the details with your own idea.**

Title _____

I think the Internet is helpful for learning in several ways.

First, _____

_____

Second, _____

_____

Lastly, _____

_____

In short, the Internet helps us _____

CHAPTER
05

UNIT 17 |

Subject Math
Topic Probability

You Are Using Probability

WARM UP

1. In what situations would you need to flip a coin?
2. How do you normally make tough decisions?

BEFORE YOU READ

A   Match the words with the definitions below.

1. _____ likelihood
2. _____ die (*n.*)
3. _____ heads
4. _____ tails
5. _____ undoubtedly
6. _____ opt

a. to choose something
b. certainly; unquestionably
c. the chance of something happening
d. the front side of a coin that has a picture on it
e. a small cube that has one to six dots on each side
f. the back side of a coin that often has a number on it

B   Background Knowledge

Probability has been in use for a long time, but it wasn't until 1654 that an official probability theory was created. Two French mathematicians, Blaise Pascal and Pierre de Fermat, came up with the theory together. They did this through letters in which they discussed the probability of winning a game of chance.

Many people dislike math, but they use it all the time. One common way people employ math is by using probability. Probability is the numerical value describing the **likelihood** that something will happen. By using probability, you can make
5 predictions about possible outcomes.

The weather forecast is one example of probability in everyday life. You have most likely heard a weather forecaster say, "There's a seventy-percent chance of rain tonight." In this case, the forecaster is using probability. What exactly does the statement mean? It
10 means that given the weather conditions tonight, seven out of ten times the result will be rain. In other words, there is a high likelihood it will rain at night.

People also use probability when they flip a coin, roll a **die**, and play the lottery. You can flip a coin to decide between two activities.
15 A coin has two sides: **heads** and **tails**. If you decide to go shopping when the coin lands on heads, then you have a fifty-fifty chance of that happening. On the other hand, there are six different numbers on a die. This means you only have a one-in-six chance of correctly predicting which number the die will land on.
20 Finally, if you are trying to guess the numbers in this week's lottery, the odds are against you. Many lotteries require that people guess six out of forty-five numbers correctly. If you calculate the possibility of winning the lottery, then you only have a one-in-8,145,060 chance
25 of that happening.

Probability is useful because it allows people to figure out whether or not they should try doing something. A businessman will **undoubtedly** start a new business with the greater odds of success.
30 A student may **opt** to major in a subject that has a greater chance of providing her with a job when she graduates. The odds for these choices—and others— can all be determined by using probability. Words 318

Q

What is the paragraph mainly about?

P1 What _____ is

P2 How probability is used to predict the _____

P3 How _____ _____, rolling a die, and playing the lottery use probability

P4 Why probability is (difficult / useful) when making decisions

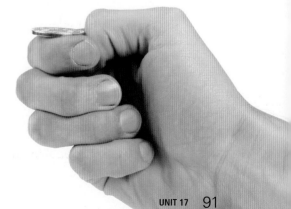

CHECK YOUR COMPREHENSION

Choose the best answers.

Main idea   1   **What is the passage mainly about?**

     a. How probability affects playing the lottery

     b. The importance of probability in weather forecasts

     c. How to calculate the probability of an event happening

     d. Ways that people use probability in their everyday lives

Details   2   **Which is NOT mentioned as a way that people use probability?**

     a. To predict the weather

     b. To decide on which activities to do

     c. To choose which college to attend

     d. To determine if a business can be successful

3   **When you roll a die, the probability of rolling each number is**

     _____.

     a. 1/2

     b. 1/3

     c. 1/4

     d. 1/6

4   **What CANNOT be inferred from the passage?**

     a. It is unlikely that a person will win the lottery.

     b. Probability is used to predict the exact time it will rain.

     c. People can make better choices by using probability.

     d. The probability of a coin landing on heads or tails is the same.

Write the answers in complete sentences.

5   **What is probability in mathematics?**

_____

6   **What does "There's a seventy-percent chance of rain tonight" mean?**

_____

SHOW YOUR COMPREHENSION

Fill in the chart with the phrases from the box.

Probability

What It Is	• ❶_____ of the likelihood that something will happen
Usage in Daily Life	• to ❷_____ in the weather forecast • to ❸_____ by flipping a coin • to determine the odds of rolling a certain number on a die • to figure out your chances of winning the lottery • to figure out if ❹_____
Why It Is Useful	• helps predict the possible outcomes so we can ❺_____

decide between two activities   we should try doing something

the numerical value   tell the chance of rain   make better choices

SUMMARIZE YOUR READING

Complete the summary with the words from the box.

chances   one-in-six   occur   winning

fifty-fifty   rolling   outcomes   weather forecast

Probability is a measure of the likelihood that an event will ❶_____ . The
❷_____ is a common way that we use probability. For example,
weather forecasters often tell us what the ❸_____ of rainy weather are.
Flipping a coin and ❹_____ a die are two other ways we use probability.
There is a ❺_____ chance of landing on heads when you flip a coin and a
❻_____ chance of predicting the correct number a die will land on. We can
also use probability to figure out our chances of ❼_____ the lottery. By using
probability, we can make predictions about possible ❽_____ , which help us
make better choices.

Subject Art & Music
Topic Caravaggio

A New Age of Painting

WARM UP
1. Who is your favorite artist?
2. What is your favorite style of art, and why?

BEFORE YOU READ

A   Match the words with the definitions below.

1. _____ tumultuous	a.	well-known or famous
2. _____ hail	b.	causing a lot of disagreement
3. _____ prowl	c.	a strong preference for something
4. _____ noted	d.	full of activity, confusion, or violence
5. _____ penchant	e.	to move around an area slowly and quietly
6. _____ controversial	f.	to draw attention to someone's achievements

B   Background Knowledge

Chiaroscuro was one of the most popular painting techniques during the Renaissance. This painting style did not focus on color but rather on light and darkness. Painters used light and dark close together in order to create a strong contrast between the two. This made the images appear as if they were three-dimensional, thus making them more realistic.

One of the greatest artists in history was born in Caravaggio, Italy, in 1571. His name was Michelangelo Merisi, but today he is known by the name of his hometown. Caravaggio had a **tumultuous** life, but he also created art that influenced countless
5　artists, including Rembrandt and Velazquez, and his works are **hailed** as masterpieces today.

Caravaggio was an angry man and was always quick to become violent. He often **prowled** the streets of Rome wearing a sword and was eager to fight anyone who offended him. In 1603, he was
10　imprisoned for a short time, and during the next few years, he had numerous legal troubles. In 1606, he committed a serious crime and was forced to flee Rome. That was not the end of his problems, for in 1608, he was imprisoned for assault but quickly escaped prison. Finally, after even more legal issues, his troubled life came
15　to an end in 1610.

Like his life, Caravaggio's paintings tended to be on the dark side. One reason for this was that he was a master of chiaroscuro. This is a painting technique that emerged during the Renaissance and involves strong contrasts between light and dark. His works
20　*The Cardsharps* and *The Crucifixion of St. Peter* are **noted** for his use of chiaroscuro.

Another prominent feature of Caravaggio's work was that he painted
25　extremely realistic pictures. For instance, he painted people with dirt underneath their fingernails and on their feet, as well as apples

▲ Basket of Fruit by Caravaggio

30　with bruises and wormholes. Caravaggio often painted scenes of a religious nature, and his **penchant** for realism was so great that many viewers were shocked by the results. Despite his **controversial** style and his trouble with the law, Caravaggio heralded a new age of painting based on realism. Thus, he is considered one of the founders of modern art. **Words 304**

Q
What is the paragraph mainly about?

P1 Who (Caravaggio / Rembrandt) was

P2 The (artistic / troubled) life of Caravaggio

P3 The painting
_____
Caravaggio mastered

P4 The _____
of Caravaggio's artworks

CHECK YOUR COMPREHENSION

Choose the best answers.

Main idea 1 **What is the passage mainly about?**

    a. Caravaggio's greatest paintings

    b. How Caravaggio got his name

    c. The life and art of Caravaggio

    d. Caravaggio's painting techniques

Details 2 **Which is NOT mentioned about Caravaggio?**

    a. He often carried a weapon with him while in Rome.

    b. He created most of his paintings in his hometown.

    c. He left Rome because he committed a crime.

    d. He committed several crimes during his life.

3 **Caravaggio's paintings were noted for** _____.

    a. their complete absence of dark colors

    b. the way that they used many different colors

    c. the brushstrokes that he used to create images

    d. the manner in which they depicted people realistically

4 **What can be inferred about Caravaggio?**

    a. He refused to try a new style of painting.

    b. He preferred to use bright colors in his work.

    c. He often painted the peaceful landscapes of his town.

    d. Not everyone loved his painting style at the time.

Write the answers in complete sentences.

5 **What is chiaroscuro?**

_____

6 **What types of realistic images did Caravaggio paint?**

_____

SHOW YOUR COMPREHENSION

Fill in the chart with the phrases from the box.

Caravaggio

Life	• born in Caravaggio, Italy • ❶ _____ that caused many problems for him • fled Rome after committing a crime
Painting Styles	• used chiaroscuro, a painting technique that creates strong ❷ _____ • painted ❸ _____
His Influence	• heralded ❹ _____ based on realism • considered one of ❺ _____

the founders of modern art   contrasts between light and dark
extremely realistic pictures   had a violent temper   a new age of painting

SUMMARIZE YOUR READING

Complete the summary with the words from the box.

many artists	committing	heralded	founders
painting technique	trouble	contrasts	violent man

Michelangelo Merisi was born in Caravaggio, Italy, in 1571 and became known to the world as simply Caravaggio. During his life, Caravaggio was a ❶ _____ and often got in ❷ _____ with the law. He even had to flee Rome after ❸ _____ a serious crime. However, he was a brilliant painter who influenced ❹ _____. Caravaggio used a ❺ _____ called chiaroscuro in his work. This technique uses ❻ _____ between light and dark. He also painted very realistic pictures. Caravaggio ❼ _____ a new age of painting and is considered one of the ❽ _____ of modern art.

UNIT 19 |
Subject Life Science
Topic The Water Cycle

Where Does the Water Go?

WARM UP

1. What happens to water when it gets very cold?
2. How does ocean water warm up?

BEFORE YOU READ

A Match the words with the definitions below.

1. _____ body of water
2. _____ droplet
3. _____ precipitation
4. _____ sleet
5. _____ hail
6. _____ penetrate

a. a very small drop of liquid
b. a lake, river, or ocean
c. a mixture of snow and rain
d. to pass through something
e. small balls of ice that fall from the clouds
f. rain, snow, or another form of water that falls to the ground

B Background Knowledge

As climate change worsens, Earth's air temperature rises. Warmer air holds more water vapor. This can cause extreme weather events, like violent rainstorms and hurricanes. When a lot of water falls at once, the ground cannot absorb it. This means dangerous floods and landslides might happen more frequently.

The water cycle is the constant movement of water on the Earth. Through this process, water travels from the Earth's surface to the atmosphere and then back to the ground again. During this cycle, water goes through three different phases; it can be a solid (ice), a
5 liquid (water), or a gas (vapor).

The water cycle begins with water vapor rising into the atmosphere through evaporation, transpiration, and sublimation. During evaporation, the sun heats water from the ground as well as **bodies of water**. As it heats, the water turns into water vapor and
10 rises. Transpiration, on the other hand, is the evaporation of water from plants. Sublimation is when solid water, like snow or ice, changes to water vapor directly.

As water vapor enters the atmosphere, it starts to cool
15 down, so condensation takes place. Condensation is the transformation of water vapor into water **droplets**. The droplets form clouds. Then, these clouds

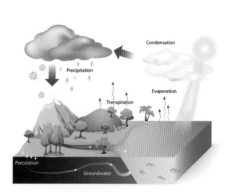

20 get heavier until they cannot hold any more water. Eventually, the water falls back to the Earth through **precipitation**. Depending on the temperature and other conditions, precipitation can take the form of rain, snow, **sleet**, or **hail**.

Water falls back into the oceans or onto the land. When it falls
25 on the land, it becomes runoff or undergoes infiltration. Runoff is water that flows into lakes, rivers, and streams and eventually goes back to the ocean. Infiltration is the process through which water soaks into the ground to create soil moisture. It might also **penetrate** the surface deeper and become groundwater. Then, the
30 water cycle takes place again.

The water cycle also affects the climate. Once water becomes vapor or clouds, the wind can move them around. They can warm or cool Earth's surface and create changes in air temperature. These factors affect the location, form, and amount of precipitation and can eventually change a region's climate. **Words 310**

Q
What is the paragraph mainly about?

P1 The main (liquids / phases) of the water cycle

P2 The ways that water turns into ___

P3 How ___ takes place

P4 Where water goes after it (falls / rises)

P5 How the water cycle affects the ___

CHECK YOUR COMPREHENSION

Choose the best answers.

Main idea 1 **What is the passage mainly about?**

a. Climate change on the Earth

b. Various forms of water on the Earth

c. The movement of water and its effects

d. Water shortage problems and their causes

Details 2 **Which is NOT true according to the passage?**

a. The water cycle has three phases.

b. Water turns into vapor when it heats up.

c. Rain, snow, and hail are forms of condensation.

d. Water becomes groundwater through infiltration.

3 **The atmosphere gets water from plants due to** _____ .

a. transpiration

b. precipitation

c. sublimation

d. infiltration

4 **What happens when clouds get too heavy to hold any more water?**

a. A larger cloud forms in the atmosphere above it.

b. The clouds break apart and then change to solids.

c. The water heats up and then evaporates quickly.

d. The water falls to the ground as precipitation.

Write the answers in complete sentences.

5 **Why does condensation take place?**

_____

6 **What happens when water that has fallen to the ground becomes runoff?**

_____

SHOW YOUR COMPREHENSION

Fill in the chart with the phrases from the box.

The Water Cycle	
Into the Atmosphere	• Evaporation: Water on the Earth changes into vapor. • Transpiration: ❶_____. • Sublimation: ❷_____ into vapor directly.
In the Atmosphere	• Condensation: Vapor ❸_____ that form clouds. • Precipitation: The water ❹_____.
On the Earth	• Runoff & Infiltration: The water that has fallen flows into the ocean or ❺_____.

water from plants changes into vapor   changes into water droplets

falls back to the Earth   becomes groundwater   solid water changes

SUMMARIZE YOUR READING

Complete the summary with the words from the box.

cools down   continuous   form clouds   the climate

water vapor   condensation   precipitation   infiltration

The water cycle is the ❶_____ movement of water. It starts when water

becomes ❷_____ through evaporation, transpiration, or sublimation.

As the vapor in the air ❸_____, it turns into water droplets through

❹_____. These droplets then ❺_____. After that, the water falls

back to the Earth through ❻_____ in the form of rain, snow, sleet, or hail. The

water that has fallen flows as runoff into the ocean or deeper into the ground, where

❼_____ occurs. Then, the water cycle begins again. The water cycle also

affects ❽_____ as wind moves vapor or clouds from one place to another.

UNIT 20 |
Subject Social Studies
Topic Singletons

The World Stays Single... Why?

WARM UP
1. Do you plan to get married when you are older?
2. Do you think teenagers should date? Why or why not?

BEFORE YOU READ

A **Match the words with the definitions below.**

1. _____ independent
2. _____ try out
3. _____ consumer
4. _____ entice
5. _____ approve of
6. _____ priority

a. to think well of something or someone
b. to persuade someone to do something
c. to do something to find out if you like it
d. not needing someone for money or help
e. something important that must be done
f. a person who buys things or uses services

B **Background Knowledge**

Families look different all over the world. In the past, many people lived in villages and worked together to raise all of the village children. In some places, this practice is still common. However, in many societies around the world, people live in what is called the nuclear family, which includes only a parent couple and their children.

A long time ago, it was common to see big families living together. In Korean culture, it was normal to have grandparents living with their sons and grandchildren. As society has developed, however, there have been many changes in families. Nowadays,

5　there are an increasing number of single-parent families as well as elderly people living by themselves.

One of the newest social units is called the singleton. Singletons are people who enjoy living alone. There are several reasons for the existence of singletons. For instance, there are now more women

10　who are economically **independent**. They no longer have to rely on men for financial security. There are also people who are focusing on their careers or studies. Additionally, some people simply put less emphasis on serious relationships.

There are a few benefits to being a singleton. People who live a

15　singleton lifestyle spend more time on personal development. Not having to financially take care of others, they have more money to spend on themselves. They are likely to use their money on fashion and beauty products to improve their looks. They also spend more time on their hobbies and **try out** new experiences like going on

20　trips.

As the number of singletons increases, various products that target them are also developing. Economists use the term solo economy to describe singletons as an emerging group of **consumers**. Indeed, home appliances and even tour packages are

25　shifting to meet the growing demands of singletons. Moreover, numerous products are **enticing** singletons to open their wallets, such as home furnishings for small spaces and miniature packets of washed rice.

Although singletons have become a

30　common phenomenon, not everyone **approves of** them. Some people view singleton life as lonely. However, it all depends on what your **priorities** are. No matter what your choice is, the most important thing is that you are content with your present lifestyle. Words 312

Q
What is the paragraph mainly about?

P1 How families have (changed / grown)

P2 What _____ are and why they exist

P3 The _____ of being a singleton

P4 How the (appliances / economy) has changed to target singletons

CHECK YOUR COMPREHENSION

Choose the best answers.

Main idea   1   **What is the passage mainly about?**

    a. Why people choose to become singletons

    b. New products that are being marketed by companies

    c. The disappearance of traditional families in modern society

    d. The causes and effects of the increasing number of singletons

Details   2   **Which is NOT mentioned as a reason for the existence of singletons?**

    a. Economic independence

    b. Emphasis on careers

    c. Continuing education

    d. Having no family

    3   **Singletons are more likely to spend their money on all of the following EXCEPT _____ .**

    a. groceries

    b. clothes

    c. beauty products

    d. vacations

    4   **What can be inferred about singletons?**

    a. They are not an influential consumer group.

    b. They prefer large homes with luxurious furniture.

    c. They are not interested in getting married.

    d. They are usually not satisfied by living alone.

Write the answers in complete sentences.

    5   **According to the passage, how have families changed as society has developed?**

_____

    6   **Why do economists use the term solo economy?**

_____

SHOW YOUR COMPREHENSION

Fill in the chart with the phrases from the box.

Singletons

Causes	• more women who are ❶_____ • people who focus on ❷_____ • people who put less emphasis on serious relationships
Lifestyles	• They spend more time and money on ❸_____, such as their looks, hobbies, and new experiences.
Effects	• The term ❹_____. • Companies are ❺_____ that target singletons.

developing various products   personal development
economically independent   their careers or studies   solo economy was created

SUMMARIZE YOUR READING

Complete the summary with the words from the box.

view   products   live alone   their jobs
financial support   being content   families   choosing

As society has changed and developed, so have the types of ❶_____.
These days, there are more people who choose to ❷_____. They are called
singletons, and there are several reasons people are increasingly ❸_____ this
lifestyle. Firstly, women no longer have to rely on men for ❹_____ and thus
have become economically independent. There are also people who are focusing on
❺_____ or studies. Singletons have more time and money to spend on
personal development. So companies are developing various ❻_____ that
target them. Some ❼_____ singletons as lonely, but ❽_____ with
your present lifestyle is all that really matters.

THINK & WRITE 5

Q **Why Do Many People in Modern Society Prefer to Spend Time Alone?**

STEP 1 **DISCUSSION** **Talk to your partner and answer the questions.**

1. What do you do when you are alone?

2. What is a benefit of being by yourself?

STEP 2 **ORGANIZATION** **Fill in the chart with the phrases from the box.**

a variety of activities	leading busy lives at school or work
relax when they are alone	other people's feelings into account
choose to do what they want	just stay home and watch movies

Introduction	These days, there are several reasons why many people prefer to spend time alone.
Body	**Supporting sentence 1:** People can _____. **Details:** _____ makes people tired, so they need to relax without being disturbed. **Supporting sentence 2:** There are _____ people can enjoy alone. **Details:** For example, they can go shopping, read a book at a café, hike by themselves, or _____. **Supporting sentence 3:** People can _____. **Details:** When they are alone, they don't need to take _____ _____. Therefore, they can make their own decisions.
Conclusion	People spend time alone because they can relax, have fun by themselves, and do the things they want.

STEP 3 `FIRST DRAFT` **Complete the writing with the phrases from the chart.**

Title Why Do Many People in Modern Society Prefer to Spend Time Alone?

These days, there are several reasons why many people prefer to spend time alone.

First, people can _____. _____ makes people tired, so they need to relax without being disturbed.

Second, there are _____ people can enjoy alone. For example, they can go shopping, read a book at a café, hike by themselves, or _____.

Lastly, people can _____. When they are alone, they don't need to take _____. Therefore, they can make their own decisions.

In short, people spend time alone because they can relax, have fun by themselves, and do the things they want.

STEP 4 `FINAL DRAFT` **Complete the writing. Replace one of the details with your own idea.**

Title _____

These days, there are several reasons why many people prefer to spend time alone.

First, _____

_____

Second, _____

_____

Lastly, _____

_____

In short, people spend time alone because they _____

_____

MEMO

MEMO

MEMO

MEMO

MEMO

School Subject-Integrated Reading Series

Reading for Subject

SECOND EDITION

Subject

Workbook

4

DARAKWON

Reading for Subject

SECOND EDITION

Workbook

4

VOCABULARY PRACTICE

A **Write the correct words for the definitions.**

observer	fame	engage in	foot traffic	beg for

1. to ask for something urgently _____

2. someone who watches something _____

3. to do something; to participate _____

4. the state of being popular or famous _____

5. the number of people walking through an area _____

B **Choose the word that has a meaning similar to the underlined word.**

1. He made most of his <u>fortune</u> in the technology industry.

   a. wealth   b. ideas   c. examples   d. exploration

2. Because she is still a student, her <u>income</u> is very low.

   a. loan   b. salary   c. employment   d. opportunity

C **Complete the sentences with the words in the box.**

clown	appealing	statue	performance	locations

1. The food tasted great and looked very _____.

2. The ballet _____ was held in the theater downtown.

3. There are three possible _____ for the city's new park.

4. It is common to hire a _____ for a child's birthday party.

5. The hospital added a stone _____ of its founder to the entrance.

I SENTENCE PRACTICE

D **Translate the sentences into your language, focusing on the meanings of the underlined parts.**

1. It wasn't until the 1860s that street performance got its name, busking.

   _____

2. Sometimes, they simply do not make enough tips to support themselves.

   _____

3. Busking offers them a means to do what they love and make a little money doing so.

   _____

4. Not everyone is friendly to buskers, and some see busking as begging for money.

   _____

E **Unscramble the words to make sentences.**

1. modern bands / their own / might / with / original songs / entertain crowds

   Similarly, _____

2. it / difficult / the music industry / do not pass / and many / auditions / can be / to break into

   For musicians, _____

3. in the form of / enjoy the performances, / offer tips / if observers / money, food, or gifts / they might

   _____

4. busking is / culture and ideas / and audience members alike / a great way / for performers / to exchange

   _____

❙ VOCABULARY PRACTICE

A **Write the correct words for the definitions.**

visually	represent	note	previous	imply

1. happening or existing before _____

2. to notice; to record something _____

3. in a way that can be seen _____

4. to suggest something in an indirect way _____

5. to present an image; to be a symbol of something _____

B **Choose the word that has a meaning similar to the underlined word.**

1. The <u>original</u> name of London was Londinium.

   a. last   b. popular   c. new   d. initial

2. They <u>split</u> the pizza into eight equal pieces and then ate it.

   a. divided   b. added   c. mashed   d. digested

C **Complete the sentences with the words in the box.**

gave birth to	petals	ratio	spiral	sum

1. The _____ of seven and eight is fifteen.

2. A golden rectangle has a _____ of 1 to 1.618.

3. His pregnant dog _____ nine little puppies.

4. A snail's shell has a _____ pattern on its back.

5. After the rain, the cherry blossom _____ fell off the tree.

❚ SENTENCE PRACTICE

D   **Translate the sentences into your language, focusing on the meanings of the underlined parts.**

1. The Fibonacci sequence is a set of numbers <u>that can be found</u> everywhere.

   _____

2. <u>When represented</u> visually, it implies that everything in life spirals outward from one source.

   _____

3. It <u>was named after</u> an Italian mathematician, Leonardo of Pisa, now <u>known as</u> Fibonacci.

   _____

4. <u>Following these assumptions</u>, the original female would give birth to a new pair at the end of the second month.

   _____

E   **Unscramble the words to make sentences.**

1. made / to solve / a few / he / the problem / assumptions

   _____

2. between / he / that / the ratio / also found / is about 1.618 / the successive numbers

   _____

3. until / the rabbits / one month old / would not / he noted that / they were / reproduce

   _____

4. the same / for the way / and the spiral shape / is true / tree branches / of a galaxy / split

   _____

VOCABULARY PRACTICE

A   **Write the correct words for the definitions.**

ceremony	symbol	regard	upper class	sake

1. a thing that represents something else   _____

2. to think of something in a specific way   _____

3. an event that includes some traditional acts   _____

4. a group of people with the highest status and wealth   _____

5. something done out of consideration for or to preserve   _____
   something

B   **Choose the word that has a meaning similar to the underlined word.**

1. Please take this <u>matter</u> up with the president of the company.

   a. issue   b. result   c. example   d. request

2. <u>Typically</u>, people in Hong Kong stay outside late at night because of the hot
   weather.

   a. Surprisingly   b. Uncommonly   c. Normally   d. Officially

C   **Complete the sentences with the words in the box.**

political	wealth	nobles	combination	is seen as

1. In China, the number four _____ a symbol of death.

2. The two parties argued with each other about _____ issues.

3. He sent her a(n) _____ of roses and daisies for her birthday.

4. Because they are _____, they are allowed to attend the royal wedding.

5. People want to be rich, but _____ does not make them happy.

▌SENTENCE PRACTICE

D   **Translate the sentences into your language, focusing on the meanings of the underlined parts.**

1. Weddings in the past <u>used to</u> be quite different from how they are nowadays.

    _____

2. Accordingly, the dresses the brides wore <u>were seen as</u> symbols of their families' wealth.

    _____

3. In Western cultures, the first wedding dresses were blue, <u>for</u> the color was seen as a symbol of purity.

    _____

4. But for many others, the color <u>has lost</u> all meaning and is merely something <u>worn</u> for tradition's sake.

    _____

E   **Unscramble the words to make sentences.**

1. the color white / regarded / then became / of wealth / wearing / as a symbol

    _____

2. because / was not / it was not / a popular option / to keep clean / an easy color

    White _____

3. to wear / from wealthy families / for brides / colorful dresses / it was also common / instead of white ones

    _____

4. wearing / in some Eastern cultures / bold color wedding dresses / and it / was natural, / still is

    Back then, _____

VOCABULARY PRACTICE

A Write the correct words for the definitions.

accessible	costly	meet	incapable	release

1. to reach; to satisfy a need _____

2. unable to do something _____

3. able to be used or got easily _____

4. expensive; requiring a lot of money _____

5. to make something available for use or purchase _____

B Choose the word that has a meaning similar to the underlined word.

1. The company tries to tackle various environmental problems.

   a. pick up   b. bring about   c. deal with   d. go ahead

2. Da Vinci often painted multiple versions of the same artwork.

   a. several   b. similar   c. colorful   d. exact

C Complete the sentences with the words in the box.

convenient	aspect	physical	embarrassing	urgently

1. I purchased the e-book instead of a(n) _____ copy.

2. He nearly lost his job due to his _____ mistake.

3. Most people feel online banking is very _____ .

4. My favorite _____ of this festival is the singing contest.

5. The message was sent _____ to warn of the hurricane.

I SENTENCE PRACTICE

D **Translate the sentences into your language, focusing on the meanings of the underlined parts.**

1. <u>As</u> many of these applications utilize AI, they <u>are capable of</u> learning.

   _____

2. Other apps can be used on smartphones to translate <u>things we see</u> in everyday life.

   _____

3. Firstly, the applications are accessible, <u>meaning</u> anyone can download and use them.

   _____

4. <u>To meet</u> the growing demand, software companies have released various translation applications.

   _____

E **Unscramble the words to make sentences.**

1. anywhere / they / taken / can be / your smartphone / you can bring

   _____

2. it is / to determine / for each language / which apps / difficult for users / are best

   _____

3. include / multiple meanings / these could / and words / cultural elements / that have

   _____

4. the software / numerous businesses / across languages / relying on / are already / to communicate

   Likewise, _____

❙ VOCABULARY PRACTICE

A   **Write the correct words for the definitions.**

satellite   oddly   asteroid   debris   atmosphere

1. strangely; unusually   _____

2. the gases that surround a planet   _____

3. an object that moves around a planet   _____

4. pieces that were broken off a larger object   _____

5. a lump of rock that orbits the sun and is smaller than   _____
    a planet

B   **Choose the word that has a meaning similar to the underlined word.**

1. They <u>assumed</u> the weather would be hot on the weekend.

    a. requested   b. explained   c. informed   d. believed

2. His paintings always include sharp lines and <u>irregular</u> shapes.

    a. round   b. oval   c. uneven   d. ordinary

C   **Complete the sentences with the words in the box.**

formation   provisional   features   gravitational fields   sphere

1. This map of the world has the shape of a _____.

2. Larger planets tend to have larger _____.

3. This hotel _____ a gym, a swimming pool, and a sauna.

4. The _____ of Earth happened around 4.5 billion years ago.

5. They haven't finished planning the event, so the date is _____.

❙ SENTENCE PRACTICE

D   **Translate the sentences into your language, focusing on the meanings of the underlined parts.**

1. However, this is untrue <u>as</u> many moons are lumpy and irregular in shape.

    _____

2. The remaining debris <u>collected to form</u> the pale, rocky sphere we now see in the night sky.

    _____

3. Also <u>known as</u> natural satellites, moons generally are solid, and most do not have an atmosphere.

    _____

4. These are moons that <u>may have been detected</u>, but scientists <u>have not been able to</u> confirm their existence.

    _____

E   **Unscramble the words to make sentences.**

1. in a wide variety / moons come / and have / of shapes / different features

    _____

2. many moons / there / orbiting / inner planets / our solar system's / aren't

    _____

3. they have / some moons / to planets / are / in that / oceans and volcanoes / similar

    _____

4. gravitational field, / to a larger / which / a larger size / pull in objects / can better / equates

    _____

▎VOCABULARY PRACTICE

A **Write the correct words for the definitions.**

tank	recipe	claim	calculation	list

1. a large container that stores a liquid _____

2. a list of instructions for making a food _____

3. to write a number of things or mention them _____

4. to say something is true, often without proof _____

5. the process of using numbers to find out an amount _____

B **Choose the word that has a meaning similar to the underlined word.**

1. <u>At times</u>, I like to be alone. Other times, I prefer to be with my friends.

   a. Rarely　　　　b. Sometimes　　　　c. After that　　　　d. Until then

2. Old technology is often thrown away because it is no longer <u>useful</u>.

   a. helpful　　　　b. useless　　　　c. worthless　　　　d. successful

C **Complete the sentences with the words in the box.**

groceries	amount	access	exact	quarter

1. Soft drinks often contain a high _____ of sugar.

2. My homework is to read the first _____ of the chapter.

3. The power went out, so we didn't have _____ to the Internet.

4. Susan makes a list of the _____ she needs before she goes to the store.

5. I don't remember the _____ address, but it was somewhere on King Street.

▌SENTENCE PRACTICE

D **Translate the sentences into your language, focusing on the meanings of the underlined parts.**

1. A decimal is simply a fraction <u>changed into</u> a number such as 0.5 or 0.75.

_____

2. <u>As</u> technology develops, some people claim <u>it</u> is not important <u>to learn</u> math.

_____

3. Imagine there are two different brands of milk <u>being sold</u> at different prices.

_____

4. We can figure out which is cheaper to buy <u>by changing</u> the total price of the milk <u>to</u> the price per liter or milliliter.

_____

_____

E **Unscramble the words to make sentences.**

1. find / to be / many people / fractions / tedious / learning

_____

2. we use / when cooking / as well / at home, / and decimals / fractions

_____

3. are / much of / for / responsible / experience / these concepts / what we

_____

4. we like to know / when we / is left / a full tank, / with less than / how much / drive a car

For example, _____

VOCABULARY PRACTICE

A **Write the correct words for the definitions.**

creation	accomplished	quit	overcome	shade

1. to stop doing something _____

2. being skilled at something _____

3. one type of a particular color _____

4. to successfully deal with or control a problem _____

5. something that was made, built, or produced _____

B **Choose the word that has a meaning similar to the underlined word.**

1. One of my friends <u>encouraged</u> me to join the baseball team.

   a. explained   b. invited   c. interfered   d. persuaded

2. The novel <u>portrays</u> the lives of penniless people living in big cities.

   a. receives   b. depicts   c. questions   d. permits

C **Complete the sentences with the words in the box.**

case	work	inspired	unforgettable	blind

1. Tony went _____ after suffering an eye injury.

2. The wedding cake she made was a real _____ of art.

3. Traveling to Africa was a(n) _____ experience for me.

4. The patient was suffering from a bad _____ of the flu.

5. Mozart's music _____ me to become a classical musician.

I SENTENCE PRACTICE

D **Translate the sentences into your language, focusing on the meanings of the underlined parts.**

1. These difficulties <u>cause</u> some people <u>to fall</u> into despair <u>while</u> they make others stronger.

   _____

2. Ray Charles, <u>one of the best-known</u> American musicians, lost his ability <u>to see</u> when he was only six.

   _____

3. <u>Being blind</u> never stopped Ray Charles from doing <u>what</u> he loved the most or from creating beautiful songs.

   _____

4. Many popular artists, musicians, and writers are remembered <u>for the way</u> they transformed their difficulties into beautiful creations.

   _____

E **Unscramble the words to make sentences.**

1. accomplished / hard work / in their fields / became / and dedication, / they

   Through _____

2. many others / difficulties / to overcome / inspire / their stories / their own

   _____

3. just like / always said / his mother / that / do anything / everyone else / he could

   _____

4. and helped / became famous / create / called soul / a new genre / he eventually / of music

   _____

VOCABULARY PRACTICE

A   **Write the correct words for the definitions.**

| mill | existence | productive | power | contribute |

1. doing or achieving a lot   _____

2. a particular way of living   _____

3. to help bring about; to help cause   _____

4. a country with a lot of influence   _____

5. a factory that makes a certain product   _____

B   **Choose the word that has a meaning similar to the underlined word.**

1. Information technology advances <u>significantly</u> every year.

    a. slightly   b. steadily   c. unfortunately   d. drastically

2. Even though he is busy supporting his family, he has a dream to <u>pursue</u>.

    a. react   b. chase   c. explain   d. ensure

C   **Complete the sentences with the words in the box.**

| abundant | monarchy | construction | deposits | urbanized |

1. New Zealand is a country famous for its _____ wildlife.

2. The country has large _____ of gold and other minerals.

3. An absolute _____ does not give any power to the people.

4. He oversaw the _____ of a new elementary school.

5. This area was _____ thanks to the new railway that was built.

▌SENTENCE PRACTICE

D   **Translate the sentences into your language, focusing on the meanings of the underlined parts.**

1.   It greatly <u>helped</u> economies <u>grow</u> and gave average people job opportunities.

_____

2.   First of all, great deposits of coal contributed to England's role <u>as</u> the birthplace of the Industrial Revolution.

_____

3.   For generations, people made their living by farming and manufacturing, <u>using</u> hand tools and simple machines.

_____

4.   More efficient steam engines <u>were developed by</u> inventors <u>through</u> the productive exchange of scientific ideas.

_____

E   **Unscramble the words to make sentences.**

1.   of the steam engine / increasing needs / led to / for the fuel / the invention

_____

2.   around the world / brought about / many / the Industrial Revolution / changes / positive

_____

3.   agriculture / for most people / the means of / the early 1700s, / existence / in England / was

Until _____

4.   another factor / influenced / the free expression / which greatly / the revolution / was / of new ideas

_____

I VOCABULARY PRACTICE

A **Write the correct words for the definitions.**

further	destruction	strike	inland	classification

1. more or to a greater degree _____

2. closer to the middle of a country _____

3. to hit; to arrive at and cause damage _____

4. the act of causing a lot of damage to something _____

5. the process of dividing things into groups _____

B **Choose the word that has a meaning similar to the underlined word.**

1. This <u>path</u> leads from the café to a beautiful beach.

   a. bridge   b. boulevard   c. driveway   d. walkway

2. The nurse helped the soldier recover from a <u>severe</u> wound.

   a. depressing   b. serious   c. healing   d. infected

C **Complete the sentences with the words in the box.**

typhoon	hit	circular	damage	accompanied

1. The tornado caused widespread _____ all across Kansas.

2. The region was _____ by a heat wave that lasted for two weeks.

3. The performers sang, clapped, and moved in a _____ motion.

4. At the news of an approaching _____, they rushed to a safe place.

5. A cold is usually _____ by a fever, a runny nose, and sneezing.

❙ SENTENCE PRACTICE

D   **Translate the sentences into your language, focusing on the meanings of the underlined parts.**

1. <u>The faster</u> the winds blow, <u>the more</u> damage a typhoon causes.

_____

2. Typhoons <u>are accompanied by</u> heavy rain and have very strong winds <u>moving</u> in a circular motion.

_____

3. <u>Once</u> a typhoon forms, it <u>tends to</u> grow stronger over warm water and weaker over cold water.

_____

4. It became <u>the worst</u> typhoon <u>ever</u> recorded to hit the country and caused the greatest amount of destruction.

_____

E   **Unscramble the words to make sentences.**

1. is / depending on / a typhoon / the speed / categorized / of its winds

_____

2. in areas / develop / over warm water / of low air pressure / many typhoons

_____

3. since it had / as a super typhoon / winds / Typhoon Haiyan / of up to 275 km/h / was classified

_____

4. in Korea / the most / with wind speeds / ever recorded / of up to / powerful typhoon / 195 km/h

It was _____

VOCABULARY PRACTICE

A   **Write the correct words for the definitions.**

garment   pesticide   toxic   landfill   fake

1. a piece of clothing   _____

2. a place where trash is dumped   _____

3. not real but appearing to be real   _____

4. harmful to living things; poisonous   _____

5. a chemical used to kill animals and insects   _____

B   **Choose the word that has a meaning similar to the underlined word.**

1. Nowadays, many <u>retailers</u> choose to advertise their products online.

   a. inventors   b. reporters   c. buyers   d. sellers

2. There was not enough <u>room</u> for the pool in the backyard.

   a. location   b. floor   c. space   d. street

C   **Complete the sentences with the words in the box.**

dyes   adopt   labor   polluter   clothing

1. The fossil fuel industry is the world's biggest _____.

2. A construction worker's job involves a lot of hard _____.

3. On Easter, they use colorful _____ to decorate boiled eggs.

4. From next year, schools will _____ an online application system.

5. The organization will donate _____ and shoes to kids in need.

❙ SENTENCE PRACTICE

D   **Translate the sentences into your language, focusing on the meanings of the underlined parts.**

1. With the invention of the sewing machine, clothing was <u>much easier</u> to produce.

    _____

2. Even natural textiles <u>made from</u> cotton are a problem <u>since</u> growing cotton uses up water resources.

    _____

3. Many are killed only <u>for</u> the garments <u>to end up</u> in a landfill when the trend changes a few months later.

    _____

4. <u>As</u> trends change fast, customers often throw away the items soon after <u>in order to</u> make room for the next trend.

    _____

E   **Unscramble the words to make sentences.**

1. of online shopping, / grown / fast fashion / the advent / has / in popularity

    With _____

2. made / the Industrial Revolution / clothing / was / the way / changed

    _____

3. into / began / clothing retailers / their designs / high fashion elements / adopting

    _____

4. pay / clothing companies / are wearing / to / what / they / careful attention

    _____

❙ VOCABULARY PRACTICE

A Write the correct words for the definitions.

ensure	associate	gain control	movement	hateful

1. to make certain _____

2. very bad or unpleasant _____

3. a person you work with; a colleague _____

4. to take over; to become the leader of something _____

5. an attempt by a group to change laws or social values _____

B Choose the word that has a meaning similar to the underlined word.

1. Critics gave the movie <u>negative</u> reviews for its weak plot.

   a. enthusiastic   b. poor   c. hurried   d. destructive

2. The <u>captive</u> became very depressed during his confinement.

   a. officer   b. prisoner   c. soldier   d. activist

C Complete the sentences with the words in the box.

mass	party	facilities	hiding	exist

1. Young kids tend to believe that ghosts really _____.

2. The _____ is working hard to win the upcoming election.

3. The school _____ are available to all of the local residents.

4. After robbing the bank, the criminal went into _____ for months.

5. The Industrial Revolution made the _____ production of goods possible.

┃ SENTENCE PRACTICE

D   **Translate the sentences into your language, focusing on the meanings of the underlined parts.**

1. Some camps had gas chambers <u>designed to</u> kill people in large numbers.

    _____

2. In her diary, she wrote about the feelings and experiences she had <u>while</u> in hiding.

    _____

3. There are memorials throughout Europe <u>where</u> concentration camps <u>used to</u> exist.

    _____

4. Long before the war, movements <u>that</u> viewed the Jewish people in a negative way <u>had begun to</u> form in Germany.

    _____

E   **Unscramble the words to make sentences.**

1. one of / the Holocaust / widely read / the most / books / it is / about

    Today, _____

2. released / many books / been / about the Holocaust / have / and films

    _____

3. Jewish people / various laws / from / to exclude / German society / were passed

    _____

4. the mass murder / was / during World War II / of Jewish Europeans / the Holocaust / by the Nazis

    _____

VOCABULARY PRACTICE

A **Write the correct words for the definitions.**

| security | heritage | geographical | landscape | cooperate |

1. an area of land that has a particular quality _____

2. the protection of a person, item, or building _____

3. relating to the land or bodies of water in an area _____

4. to work with other people to achieve a goal _____

5. things from the past that have cultural or historical importance _____

B **Choose the word that has a meaning similar to the underlined word.**

1. Advances in medicine have benefited <u>humankind</u> in many ways.

   a. people   b. animals   c. resources   d. nature

2. Climate change is a <u>universal</u> problem because it affects us all.

   a. unimportant   b. widespread   c. critical   d. unfortunate

C **Complete the sentences with the words in the box.**

| monument | civilization | categorized | extraordinary | registered |

1. The store _____ the books according to their genre.

2. His incredible research generated some _____ results.

3. The Mayans were a _____ that lived in what is now Mexico.

4. The _____ was built in memory of the school's founder last year.

5. You have not _____ for any classes yet, so make sure to do that soon.

▌SENTENCE PRACTICE

D **Translate the sentences into your language, focusing on the meanings of the underlined parts.**

1. The dam <u>would have flooded</u> an important site from ancient Egyptian civilization.

   _____

2. The last type is mixed heritage<u>, which</u> includes sites with <u>both</u> cultural <u>and</u> natural value.

   _____

3. <u>Believing</u> that culture plays a role in human development, UNESCO has worked hard <u>to protect</u> World Heritage Sites.

   _____

4. UNESCO believes they belong to all of us <u>rather than</u> to any one nation, so they <u>should be saved</u> for future generations.

   _____

E **Unscramble the words to make sentences.**

1. has / on the list / cultural heritage sites / South Korea / registered / numerous

   _____

2. these heritage sites / or physical / a special cultural / have / significance / to humankind

   _____

3. in 2007 / it became / an extraordinary / a natural heritage site / and boasts / volcanic landscape

   _____

4. to a higher place / to relocate / the purpose / was / of the campaign / the Great Temple of Abu Simbel

   _____

VOCABULARY PRACTICE

A   **Write the correct words for the definitions.**

regardless of   vomit   deem   disorder   weigh

1. to have a certain heaviness _____

2. without being affected by _____

3. to consider something in a certain way _____

4. a health problem, either mental or physical _____

5. to release the stomach's contents through the mouth _____

B   **Choose the word that has a meaning similar to the underlined word.**

1. The college will <u>restrict</u> the number of applicants to 800.

    a. present   b. mimic   c. invite   d. limit

2. Doctors recommend that you eat eight <u>portions</u> of vegetables.

    a. selections   b. collections   c. servings   d. groups

C   **Complete the sentences with the words in the box.**

pressured   underweight   overeating   purge   biological

1. Low calorie diets often lead to periods of _____.

2. The puppies must eat more because they're _____.

3. Teenagers often feel _____ to dress like their peers.

4. Mary is adopted, but she wants to find her _____ father.

5. The patient took pills to _____ the food from her body.

❙ SENTENCE PRACTICE

D   **Translate the sentences into your language, focusing on the meanings of the underlined parts.**

1. This in turn <u>causes them to</u> become dangerously underweight and may even result in death.

    _____

2. Some experts point to <u>the way</u> young women are portrayed in the media <u>as</u> a possible cause.

    _____

3. People <u>suffering</u> from anorexia nervosa often believe they are overweight <u>regardless of</u> how much they actually weigh.

    _____

4. Instead of limiting food intake, people <u>who</u> suffer from bulimia nervosa may go through periods <u>where</u> they eat large amounts of food.

    _____

E   **Unscramble the words to make sentences.**

1. relationship / people / an unhealthy / who have eating disorders / have / with food

    _____

2. from their bodies / also use / the food / they might / to quickly flush / medicines

    _____

3. social factors / it / several / could / biological and / psychologists believe / be

    However, _____

4. by / the disordered / be restricted / that / is caused / food intake / should / belief

    Bulimia nervosa _____

VOCABULARY PRACTICE

A **Write the correct words for the definitions.**

reunite	suggest	flaw	play	royalty

1. to come together again _____

2. a weakness or defect in something _____

3. to mention or propose something _____

4. kings, queens, and their family members _____

5. a stage performance with actors and costumes _____

B **Choose the word that has a meaning similar to the underlined word.**

1. Many children enjoy the <u>plot</u> of *Snow White and the Seven Dwarfs*.

   a. characters   b. storyline   c. twists   d. setting

2. The problem was so <u>complex</u> that she couldn't understand it.

   a. complicated   b. troublesome   c. frightening   d. important

C **Complete the sentences with the words in the box.**

subject matter	turn	refer to	classified	revenge

1. The _____ of a horror movie can be terrifying.

2. The prince got _____ after his kingdom was invaded.

3. The giant panda is _____ as an endangered species.

4. We did not like the strange _____ the story took at the end.

5. These numbers _____ the atomic number of each element.

┃ SENTENCE PRACTICE

D   **Translate the sentences into your language, focusing on the meanings of the underlined parts.**

1.   The term comedy does not have the same meaning it <u>does</u> today.

2.   This means the hero has some sort of flaw <u>that ends up causing</u> his or her death.

3.   For example, the main character may seem like a tragic hero only <u>for</u> the story <u>to have</u> a happy ending.

4.   <u>Unlike</u> his comedies, Shakespeare's tragedies usually feature nobility and royalty, and the main character is usually considered a tragic hero.

E   **Unscramble the words to make sentences.**

1.   the plots / surprising twists / many / complex / with / are / and turns

2.   and performed / to this day, / are still / all around the world / studied / his plays

3.   always agree on / do not / be considered / what can / critics / a tragicomedy

4.   Shakespeare's tragedies / more serious / and the difference / subject matter, / focus on / such as revenge / between good and evil

VOCABULARY PRACTICE

A **Write the correct words for the definitions.**

ideal	compelling	boost	punishment	mature

1. exciting and interesting _____

2. perfect; most suitable _____

3. to grow older and wiser _____

4. to increase or improve something _____

5. the act of making someone suffer for something _____

B **Choose the word that has a meaning similar to the underlined word.**

1. Her pain was so severe that she needed <u>immediate</u> treatment.

    a. bright   b. professional   c. quick   d. extreme

2. John was <u>motivated</u> to be a scientist thanks to his professor's lecture.

    a. driven   b. asked   c. reminded   d. trained

C **Complete the sentences with the words in the box.**

flexibility	got used to	suggestions	democratic	matters

1. The key to success is _____ and hard work.

2. My boss turned down some of my _____.

3. What _____ to me is that you are happy and healthy.

4. The little girl _____ being treated like a princess.

5. In a _____ country, all adult citizens have the right to vote.

I SENTENCE PRACTICE

D **Translate the sentences into your language, focusing on the meanings of the underlined parts.**

1. Some believe certain people were born with the skills <u>needed to become</u> compelling leaders.

_____

2. As a result, they might do the minimum amount of work <u>expected</u> of them <u>to avoid</u> penalties.

_____

3. This method works when the rewards and punishments are <u>what</u> motivate the people <u>involved</u>.

_____

4. This type of leadership boosts the members' morale <u>since</u> they can <u>make</u> their voices <u>heard</u> in the decision-making process.

_____

E **Unscramble the words to make sentences.**

1. it / as if / them / feel / makes / matter / their opinions

_____

2. it may cause / to get used to / people / are told / what they / to do / doing only

_____

3. not / it is / needs to / an ideal choice / when an organization / make a quick decision

_____

4. force / coercive leaders / their team members / by threatening them / their orders / to follow / with punishment

Next, _____

VOCABULARY PRACTICE

A Write the correct words for the definitions.

application	undergo	appearance	wounded	constantly

1 to experience something

_____

2. the state of having an injury

_____

3. how someone or something looks

_____

4. without stopping; always

_____

5. a way in which something can be used

_____

B Choose the word that has a meaning similar to the underlined word.

1. The passengers on the plane <u>reacted</u> quickly when they heard the alarm.

a. panicked   b. responded   c. observed   d. fled

2. We used this striped <u>fabric</u> to create all of the curtains in the living room.

a. patch   b. padding   c. cloth   d. glass

C Complete the sentences with the words in the box.

materials	electronic	stabilize	monitor	warned

1. This device is used to constantly _____ a patient's heart rate.

2. I cannot wear synthetic _____ because of my skin problems.

3. This vacuum cleaner has many complex _____ components.

4. The fire alarm _____ the apartment residents that there was a fire.

5. The doctor prescribed some drugs that will _____ the patient's mind.

┃ SENTENCE PRACTICE

D **Translate the sentences into your language, focusing on the meanings of the underlined parts.**

1. If a soldier gets wounded or sick, the uniform <u>makes it easier to</u> stabilize him or her.

   _____

2. They are fabrics <u>that</u> have electronic materials, such as computer chips, <u>embedded</u> in them.

   _____

3. <u>As</u> smart textiles continue to improve, they <u>will likely</u> have many more applications in the future.

   _____

4. When the temperature gets warmer, the smart textiles alter the clothes in some way <u>so that</u> they make the wearer cooler.

   _____

E **Unscramble the words to make sentences.**

1. the clothing / people / what / is going to / of the future / often wonder / be like

   _____

2. soldiers / protect / heat, dangerous chemicals, / these uniforms / and gases / from

   _____

3. are about / the wearers / if they / will warn / any problems, / to experience / the clothes

   _____

4. is cold, / the wearer / the material undergoes / warm / when the temperature / to help keep / some changes

   _____

❙ VOCABULARY PRACTICE

A   **Write the correct words for the definitions.**

prediction	condition	outcome	graduate	calculate

1. the result of something _____

2. to finish school and receive a diploma _____

3. the state of something, such as the weather _____

4. to use numbers to find out a number, answer, etc. _____

5. a statement about what you think is going to happen _____

B   **Choose the word that has a meaning similar to the underlined word.**

1. It is impossible to improve your <u>odds</u> of winning this game.

   a. chances   b. incidents   c. changes   d. expressions

2. To <u>employ</u> your time wisely, you should make a schedule for each day.

   a. adjust   b. slow   c. inform   d. use

C   **Complete the sentences with the words in the box.**

numerical	major in	statement	lottery	flipped

1. After Timmy won the _____, he lived in luxury.

2. The books in the library are organized in _____ order.

3. They _____ a coin to see who would wash the dishes.

4. There was an official _____ about the presidential election.

5. My brother decided to _____ engineering when he goes to college.

❙ SENTENCE PRACTICE

D   **Translate the sentences into your language, focusing on the meanings of the underlined parts.**

1.   Probability is the numerical value <u>describing</u> the likelihood <u>that</u> something will happen.

_____

2.   It means that <u>given</u> the weather conditions tonight, seven out of ten times the result will be rain.

_____

3.   This means you only have a one-in-six chance of correctly predicting <u>which number</u> the die will land on.

_____

4.   A student may opt to major in a subject <u>that</u> has a greater chance of <u>providing</u> her <u>with</u> a job when she graduates.

_____

E   **Unscramble the words to make sentences.**

1.   in other words, / is / rain / likelihood / there / at night / a high / it will

_____

2.   math / people / employ / is / one common way / probability / by using

_____

3.   that / people guess / six / many lotteries / out of / require / forty-five numbers correctly

_____

4.   to figure out / is useful / doing something / because / whether or not / it allows people / they should try

Probability _____

I VOCABULARY PRACTICE

A   **Write the correct words for the definitions.**

founder   contrast   countless   flee   sword

1. very many; too many to count   _____

2. a difference between two or more things   _____

3. a large blade with a handle, used for fighting   _____

4. to leave a place very quickly to escape danger   _____

5. someone who starts an organization, trend, etc.   _____

B   **Choose the word that has a meaning similar to the underlined word.**

1. She noticed the area had many <u>prominent</u> landmarks.

    a. important   b. former   c. unknown   d. expensive

2. He <u>offended</u> the vice president with his rude behavior.

    a. informed   b. confirmed   c. insulted   d. convinced

C   **Complete the sentences with the words in the box.**

masterpieces   assault   religious   heralded   committed

1. He was arrested because he had _____ a crime.

2. The man was charged with _____, and he is still in prison.

3. The *Mona Lisa* is considered to be one of Da Vinci's _____.

4. The right to _____ freedom is not guaranteed in some countries.

5. The digital age has _____ a new way of learning and communicating.

SENTENCE PRACTICE

D **Translate the sentences into your language, focusing on the meanings of the underlined parts.**

1. He often prowled the streets of Rome wearing a sword and was eager to fight anyone <u>who</u> offended him.

   _____

2. This is a painting technique <u>that</u> emerged during the Renaissance and involves strong contrasts <u>between</u> light <u>and</u> dark.

   _____

3. His penchant for realism was <u>so great that</u> many viewers were shocked by the results.

   _____

4. <u>Despite</u> his controversial style and his trouble with the law, Caravaggio heralded a new age of painting <u>based on</u> realism.

   _____

E **Unscramble the words to make sentences.**

1. committed / forced to / crime / he / and was / flee Rome / a serious

   In 1606, _____

2. an angry man / to become / Caravaggio / always quick / was / and was / violent

   _____

3. he also / but / Caravaggio had / that influenced / created art / countless artists / a tumultuous life,

   _____

4. that / of Caravaggio's work / was / pictures / he painted / another prominent feature / extremely realistic

   _____

❙ VOCABULARY PRACTICE

A **Write the correct words for the definitions.**

| region | evaporation | go through | heat | surface |

1. an area of land _____

2. to experience something _____

3. the top layer of something _____

4. when water changes into a vapor _____

5. to make something hot or warm _____

B **Choose the word that has a meaning similar to the underlined word.**

1. The main <u>factor</u> of success is how efficiently a plan works.

   a. change   b. cause   c. event   d. invention

2. We see the moon in different <u>phases</u> throughout the month.

   a. aspects   b. places   c. stages   d. incidents

C **Complete the sentences with the words in the box.**

| atmosphere | soaked into | depending on | sublimation | vapor |

1. Living expenses vary _____ the area you live in.

2. The orange juice I spilled _____ the mat and stained it.

3. Dry ice disappears due to a process called _____.

4. Cars release harmful greenhouse gases into the _____.

5. You can see water _____ when you breathe out on a cold day.

❚ SENTENCE PRACTICE

D   **Translate the sentences into your language, focusing on the meanings of the underlined parts.**

1. Then, these clouds <u>get heavier until</u> they cannot hold any more water.

_____

2. <u>Depending on</u> the temperature and other conditions, precipitation can take the form of rain, snow, sleet, or hail.

_____

3. Infiltration is the process <u>through which</u> water soaks into the ground <u>to create</u> soil moisture.

_____

4. <u>As</u> water vapor enters the atmosphere, it <u>starts to</u> cool down, so condensation takes place.

_____

E   **Unscramble the words to make sentences.**

1. on the Earth / the water cycle / the constant / is / of water / movement

_____

2. water droplets / into / the transformation / condensation is / of water vapor

_____

3. once water / can move / becomes / around / vapor or clouds, / the wind / them

_____

4. water from the ground / during evaporation, / as well / heats / as bodies of water / the sun

_____

VOCABULARY PRACTICE

A   **Write the correct words for the definitions.**

unit   furnishing   target   normal   emerging

1. usual, typical, or expected   _____

2. starting to exist or become known   _____

3. to direct something toward someone   _____

4. furniture; something used to decorate a home _____

5. a single thing, often separate from something larger _____

B   **Choose the word that has a meaning similar to the underlined word.**

1. Mike decided to quit his job because he was not <u>content</u> with it.

    a. happy   b. impressed   c. disappointed   d. displeased

2. The company will <u>shift</u> its marketing plans to reach teenagers.

    a. destroy   b. employ   c. prepare   d. change

C   **Complete the sentences with the words in the box.**

appliances   financial   economically   emphasis   personal

1. North Korea is _____ dependent on South Korea.

2. To achieve _____ security, I asked my boss for a raise.

3. Many people learn new languages for _____ development.

4. You can save energy by unplugging _____ after using them.

5. The new government put more _____ on the welfare of the people.

I SENTENCE PRACTICE

D   **Translate the sentences into your language, focusing on the meanings of the underlined parts.**

1. Economists use the term solo economy <u>to describe</u> singletons <u>as</u> an emerging group of consumers.

2. <u>Not having to</u> financially take care of others, they have more money to spend on themselves.

3. <u>Although</u> singletons have become a common phenomenon, <u>not everyone</u> approves of them.

4. <u>No matter what</u> your choice is, the most important thing is <u>that</u> you are content with your present lifestyle.

E   **Unscramble the words to make sentences.**

1. it / to see / big families / common / was / living together

2. have to / men / they / for financial security / no longer / rely on

3. emphasis / some people / serious relationships / less / on / simply put

    Additionally, _____

4. on fashion / they are / their looks / their money / likely to use / and beauty products / to improve

MEMO

MEMO

MEMO

MEMO

Reading for Subject

SECOND EDITION